THE PILLARS OF SOCIETY

D1439149

The Plays of Ibsen

(1828–1906)

with their dates of composition

CATILINE, 1849
THE WARRIOR'S BARROW, 1849–50
NORMA, 1851
ST JOHN'S EVE, 1852
LADY INGER OF OESTRAAT, 1854
THE FEAST AT SOLHAUG, 1855
OLAF LILJEKRANS, 1856
THE VIKINGS AT HELGELAND, 1857
LOVE'S COMEDY, 1862
THE PRETENDERS, 1863
BRAND, 1865
PEER GYNT, 1867
THE LEAGUE OF YOUTH, 1868–69
EMPEROR AND GALILEAN, 1864–73
THE PILLARS OF SOCIETY, 1875–77
A DOLL'S HOUSE, 1879
GHOSTS, 1881
AN ENEMY OF THE PEOPLE, 1882
THE WILD DUCK, 1884
ROSMERSHOLM, 1886
THE LADY FROM THE SEA, 1888
HEDDA GABLER, 1890
THE MASTER BUILDER, 1892
LITTLE EYOLF, 1894
JOHN GABRIEL BORKMAN, 1896
WHEN WE DEAD AWAKEN, 1899

HENRIK IBSEN

The Pillars of Society

NEWLY TRANSLATED FROM THE NORWEGIAN BY

Michael Meyer

RUPERT HART-DAVIS

Soho Square London

1963

PRINTED IN GREAT BRITAIN
BY WESTERN PRINTING SERVICES LTD BRISTOL

CONTENTS

INTRODUCTION

Ibsen completed *The Pillars of Society* a few months after his forty-ninth birthday; he wrote it in Munich between 1875 and 1877. Enormously successful and influential at the time of its appearance, and indeed for the next quarter of a century, it has rarely been performed during the past fifty years, having rather glibly been relegated to the category of polemical dramas that have lost their topicality. It is customarily thought of nowadays as an apprentice work of documentary rather than practical interest. In fact, however, the whole question of which plays of Ibsen are still theatrically valid is in serious need of reappraisal. Recent productions in London of *Brand* and *Little Eyolf*, which had both long been dismissed as unactable, have shown them to be full of theatrical life, and the same is probably true of *The Pillars of Society*. It is tightly plotted and beautifully characterized; and at this distance of time we can see that its true subject is not women's rights or the evil practices of nineteenth-century shipowners, but human emotions and relationships. The ending has been condemned as facilely happy, but the same accusation was, until recently, made against *Little Eyolf* and *The Lady from the Sea*, and has been proved false if the plays are capably handled. The chief obstacles to a professional production are the size of the cast and a tendency to verbosity on the part of Bernick and, more particularly, Dr Roerlund the schoolmaster. Trim them down, and *The Pillars of Society* stands as an absorbing example of Ibsen in his less familiar mood of humane comedy —the mood which pervades *Love's Comedy*, *The League of Youth* and much of *Peer Gynt* and *The Wild Duck*, and of which isolated characters in his more sombre plays, such as

7

George Tesman in *Hedda Gabler*, Ballested in *The Lady from the Sea*, and Vilhelm Foldal in *John Gabriel Borkman*, are belated manifestations.

The Pillars of Society is often referred to as the first of Ibsen's social prose dramas. That honour in fact belongs to *The League of Youth*, a vigorous and delightful comedy completed eight years earlier which hardly deserves the oblivion which has enveloped it. To *The League of Youth*, too, belongs the credit of being Ibsen's first attempt to write dialogue that was genuinely modern and colloquial. His earlier prose plays, such as *St John's Eve*, *Lady Inger of Oestraat*, *The Vikings at Helgeland* and *The Pretenders*, had been written in a formalized style. But *The League of Youth*, often assumed by those who have not read it to be an earnest political tract, is a loosely constructed and light-hearted frolic almost in the manner of Restoration comedy,[1] which happens to have a pushing young politician as its chief character—"Peer Gynt as a politician," someone has described it. *The Pillars of Society* is in a much truer sense the forerunner of the eleven great plays which followed it. Apart from the tightness of its construction, it contains, as *The League of Youth* does not, the elements we commonly associate with an Ibsen play—a marriage founded on a lie, passionate women stunted and inhibited by the conventions of their time, and an arrogant man of high intellectual and practical gifts who destroys, or nearly destroys, the happiness of those nearest to him. It also exhibits, unlike his earlier plays, what Henry James admiringly described as "the operation of talent without glamour . . . the ugly interior on which his curtain inexorably rises and which, to be honest, I like for the queer associations it has taught us to respect: the hideous carpet and wallpaper (one may answer for them), the conspicuous stove, the lonely central table, the 'lamps with green shades' as in the sumptuous first act of *The Wild Duck*, the pervasive air of small interests and standards, the sign of limited local life." Above all, *The Pillars of Society* has, despite its overtones of comedy, that peculiarly Ibsenish quality of

---

[1] It was influenced by the eighteenth-century Danish dramatist Ludvig Holberg, one of the few authors Ibsen really admired.

8

austerity; what Henry James, on another occasion, described as "the hard compulsion of his strangely inscrutable art."

It is indicative of the technical problems posed by this new form of tightly plotted social realism that *The Pillars of Society* took Ibsen longer to write than any of his other plays except the triple-length *Emperor and Galilean*. No less than five separate drafts of the first act have survived, and over a period of nearly eight years his letters are scattered with excuses for its lack of progress. He began to brood on it as early as December 1869, just after finishing *The League of Youth*. On the fourteenth of that month he wrote to his publisher Frederik Hegel: "I am planning a new and serious contemporary drama in three acts, and expect to start work on it in the immediate future." The following month (25 January 1870) he informed Hegel that he hoped to have it ready by the following October, but on 11 April he wrote: "My new play has not yet got beyond the draft, and since I have to get my travel notes into order it looks like being delayed for some time." These travel notes referred to the visit he had made to Egypt in November 1869 to attend, as official Norwegian representative, the opening of the Suez Canal.

October 1870 arrived, and so far from having the play ready he could only tell Hegel that it "has sufficiently developed in my mind for me to hope that any day now I may be able to start writing it." Two sets of notes have survived from this year which contain the first germs of the play. By now he had found a more impressive excuse than the Suez Canal: the Franco-Prussian War, which had started in July of that year. In such an atmosphere (he was living in Germany) how could he concentrate on writing a social drama set in a small Norwegian seaport? He returned instead to the broader historical canvas of *Emperor and Galilean*, on which he had been working intermittently since 1864.

It was in fact another five years before he began the actual writing of *The Pillars of Society*. Apart from completing *Emperor and Galilean*, he prepared for publication a selection of his poems covering the past twenty years; it was his deliberate farewell to poetry, the form which had been his earliest love. He explained this decision in a letter written to Edmund Gosse on 15 January 1874, shortly after the publication of *Emperor and Galilean*, and although his remarks were made with specific reference to that play, they apply even more strongly to the works which followed. I quote the passage in Gosse's own translation:

"The illusion I wanted to produce is that of reality. I wished to produce the impression on the reader that what he was reading was something that had really happened. If I had employed verse, I should have counteracted my own intention and prevented the accomplishment of the task I had set myself. The many ordinary and insignificant characters whom I have introduced into the play would have become indistinct, and indistinguishable from one another, if I had allowed all of them to speak in one and the same rhythmical measure. We are no longer living in the age of Shakespeare. Among sculptors, there is already talk of painting statues in the natural colours. Much can be said both for and against this. I have no desire to see the Venus de Milo painted, but I would rather see the head of a negro executed in black than in white marble.

"Speaking generally, the style must conform to the degree of ideality which pervades the representation. My new drama [*Emperor and Galilean*] is no tragedy in the ancient acceptation; what I desired to depict were human beings, and therefore I would not let them talk in 'the language of the gods.' "

In the summer of 1874 Ibsen returned to Norway for the first time since he had left it ten years earlier. There the strife between the conservatives and the liberals had reached its height and, as a result of *The League of Youth*, which was an attack on the hollowness of radical politicians, Ibsen found the conservatives hailing him as their champion. He had, however, no intention of attaching himself to any political party, and when he read in the right-wing newspaper *Morgenbladet* an editorial demand that a candidate for a professorship at the University should be rejected on the grounds that he was a freethinker, Ibsen seized the opportunity to advertise his independence. He withdrew his subscription to *Morgenbladet* and changed to the left-wing newspaper *Dagbladet*. The uneasiness of the conservatives on hearing this—Ibsen was famous enough by now for the students to arrange a torchlight procession in his honour before he left—would have been considerably increased if they had known what he was preparing for them.

After two and a half months in Norway, he returned briefly to Dresden and then, the following spring (1875), he moved to Munich, a city which he found much more to his liking and where he was to spend most of the next sixteen years. At last, in the autumn of that year, nearly six years after he had first begun to brood on it, he settled down to the actual writing of *The Pillars of Society*. At first things went well. On 23 October he wrote to Hegel: "My new play is progressing swiftly; in a few days I shall have completed the first act, which I always find the most difficult part. The title will be: *The Pillars of Society*, a Play in Five [*sic*] Acts. In a way it can be regarded as a counterblast to *The League of Youth*, and will touch on several of the more important questions of our time." On 25 November he writes: "Act 1 of my new play is finished and *fair-copied*; I am now working on Act 2." By 10 December he is "working at it daily and am now doubly anxious to get the manuscript to you as quickly as possible." On 26 January 1876 he expects to "have it ready by May."

But now things began to go less smoothly. After 26 February, when he writes to the director of the Bergen Theatre that it "will probably be printed during the summer," there is no further mention of the play in his letters until 15 September, when he explains rather lengthily to Hegel that he has been so distracted by productions or plans for productions of his earlier plays—*The Pretenders* in Meiningen, Schwerin and Berlin, *The Vikings at Helgeland* in Munich, Leipzig, Vienna and Dresden—that he has been "compelled to postpone completion of my new play; but on my return to Munich at the beginning of next month, I intend to get it polished off." But progress continued to be slow. 1877 arrived, and on 9 February he could only tell Hegel, who must by now have been growing a little impatient: "I shall have my new play ready in the summer, and will send you the manuscript as soon as possible." However, on 20 April he wrote that it "is now moving rapidly towards its conclusion," and at last, on 24 June 1877, he was able to report: "Today I take advantage of a free moment to tell you that on the 15th inst. I completed my new play and am now going ahead with the fair-copying." He posted the fair copy to Hegel in five instalments between 29 July and 20 August 1877.

The Pillars of Society was published by Hegel's firm, Gyldendals of Copenhagen, on 11 October 1877, and achieved immediate and widespread success. Throughout Scandinavia, the liberals and radicals hailed it with as much delight as that with which the conservatives had greeted *The League of Youth*. The first edition of 6,000 copies sold out in seven weeks, and a further 4,000 had to be printed. It was first performed on 18 November 1877 in Copenhagen, where it was received with great enthusiasm, and it was equally acclaimed in Christiania,[1] Stockholm and Helsinki. It also gave Ibsen his first real breakthrough in Germany. In the absence of any copyright protection, three separate German translations were published early in 1878 (one of them by a man described by Ibsen as "a frightful literary bandit"), and in February of that year it was produced at five different theatres in Berlin within a fortnight. Twenty-seven German and Austrian theatres staged it within the year. In England, William Archer, then aged twenty-two, made a "hurried translation" entitled, rather uninspiringly, *The Supports of Society*; an analysis by him of the play, with extracts from his translation, was published in the *Mirror of Literature* on 2 March 1878. Since "no publisher would look at" this version, he made another and more careful one, under the new title of *Quicksands*, and this was performed for a single matinée at the Gaiety Theatre, London, on 15 December 1880—a noteworthy occasion, for it was the first recorded performance of any Ibsen play in

[1] In Swedish at the Moellergaten Theatre. Ibsen refused to allow the Christiania Theatre to stage it because "the new director is a quite useless man," and the play was not performed in Norwegian in the capital until the following spring.

England. *The Pillars of Society* was not staged in America, at any rate in English—though it had been acted there in German—until 13 March 1891, when it was produced at the Lyceum Theatre, New York. In 1892 it was performed in Australia and South Africa, in 1893 in Rome; and in 1896 Lugné-Poe staged it at his Théâtre de l'Œuvre in Paris. By the end of the century, according to Archer, it had been performed no less than 1,200 times in Germany and Austria, a remarkable record for those days.

The Pillars of Society dealt with two problems of extreme topicality for the eighteen-seventies, and it is a measure of the play's emotional and dramatic content that it has retained its validity despite the fact that both issues have long since been settled. One was the question of women's rights; the other, that of "floating coffins," i.e. unseaworthy ships which were deliberately sacrificed with their crews so that their owners could claim insurance. Controversy over the former problem reached its height in Norway during the seventies. The Norwegian novelist Camilla Collett had fired a warning shot as early as 1853, with her novel *The Judge's Daughters*. In 1869 John Stuart Mill published *The Subjection of Women*, which Ibsen's friend Georg Brandes translated into Danish the same year. Matilda Schjoett's *Conversation of a Group of Ladies about the Subjection of Women* (published anonymously in 1871) and Camilla Collett's *Last Papers* (1872) set the issue squarely before the Norwegian public; in 1874 a Women's Reading Society was founded in Christiania, and in 1876 Asta Hanseen, a great champion of the cause, began a series of lectures on women's rights, but was so furiously assailed that in 1880 she emigrated to America. She was the original of Lona Hessel (Ibsen at first gave the character the surname of Hassel, but changed it, presumably so as to avoid too direct an identification with Hanseen). Camilla Collett exerted a direct influence on Ibsen, for he had seen a good deal of her in Dresden in 1871, and again in Munich in the spring of 1877 when he was writing the play, and when they had many arguments about marriage and other female problems. Another influence

13

was Ibsen's wife Susannah; the subject of women's rights was one about which she had long felt strongly. Ibsen had already touched tentatively on this problem in *The League of Youth*, and he was to deal with it more minutely in his next play, *A Doll's House*. His original intention in *The Pillars of Society* was to be even more outspoken than he finally was, for in one of the preliminary drafts Dina announces her decision to go off with her lover without marrying him; but he evidently doubted whether the theatres would stage a play which suggested anything quite so daring, and legalized their relationship.

The problem of the "floating coffins" was first forced upon Ibsen's attention by an English Member of Parliament. In 1868 Samuel Plimsoll had sought in the House of Commons to have the State interfere against the cold-blooded and un-scrupulous sacrifice of human life by sending men to sea in rotten ships. In 1873 he succeeded in getting a law passed to enforce seaworthiness; but this proved too slack. On 22 July 1875 he created a tremendous commotion in Parliament by a boldly outspoken attack on the people responsible for such a policy; he called the owners of such ships murderers and the politicians who supported them scoundrels. This so roused the conscience of the nation that a temporary bill went through in a few days, and its principles were made permanent by the Merchant Shipping Act of the following year. Plimsoll's pro-test echoed throughout the world, and in a seafaring country such as Norway it rang especially loudly. A particularly scan-dalous case had occurred in Christiania during Ibsen's visit there in 1874. On 2 September of that year, at the annual general meeting of the shipping insurance company Norske Veritas, questions were asked about a ship which, after having been declared seaworthy, sprang a leak while at sea and was shown to be completely rotten. At the annual general meeting a year later two similar cases were mentioned, and a storm of indignation was aroused. The matter was reported in detail in the newspapers, and Ibsen can hardly have failed to read about it.

The Pillars of Society is full of memories of Grimstad, the little port where Ibsen had spent his years as a chemist's apprentice (just as *The League of Youth* is full of memories of his birthplace, Skien). The *Palm Tree* was the name of a Grimstad ship. Touring theatrical companies played in the hall of a sailmaker named Moeller; an actress belonging to one of them had returned there after being involved in a scandal, and had tried to keep herself by taking in washing and sewing like Dina Dorf's mother, but had been shooed out of town by the local gossips. Foreign ships came in for repairs, and foreign visitors turned the place upside-down, like the crew of the *Indian Girl*. In the autumn of 1849, six months before Ibsen left for Christiania, the Socialist Marcus Thrane had arrived in Grimstad and founded a Workers' Association, like the one Aune belonged to. And the Bernicks had their origin in a family named Smith Petersen. Morten Smith Petersen, the original of Karsten Bernick, returned to Grimstad from abroad in the eighteen-forties, and ran his aged mother's business for a while, but finally had to close it down. He then started his own shipyard and an insurance company, and eventually founded the Norske Veritas company which earned the notoriety referred to above. He had died in 1872, but his sister Margrethe Petersen survived. She was an elementary schoolteacher, and was the original of Martha Bernick.

The rich quantity of notes and draft material which has been preserved enables us to plot the development of *The Pillars of Society* in some detail. His first notes, made in 1870, begin: "The main theme must be how women sit modestly in the background while the men busily pursue their petty aims with an assurance which at once infuriates and impresses." The main characters are to be an "old white-haired lady" with two sons, one a shipowner, the other a ship's officer who has been abroad for ten years on foreign service. The shipowner's wife, "a fêted beauty before she married, is full of poetry but is bitter and unsatisfied; she makes demands of life which are, or seem, excessive." In other words, Mrs Bernick, as originally conceived, is a forerunner of the great line of Ibsen heroines—Nora Hellmer, Mrs Alving, Rebecca West, Ellida Wangel, Hedda Gabler, Rita Allmers, the Rentheim twins in *John Gabriel Borkman*, and Maja and Irene in *When We Dead Awaken*. Martha, too, appears in these early notes, jotted down five years before the play was written: "her sister, still unsure of herself; has grown up quietly admiring the man who is absent and far away." But although several of the characters of *The Pillars of Society* as we know it are here, the plot as originally conceived bears little relation to that of the final version; the naval officer falls in love with the sister (i.e., Martha), but she is already in love with a student, and the officer's mother persuades him to give up the girl and go away. "The greatest victory," she tells him, "is to conquer oneself" —a kind of echo of Brand's "The victory of victories is to lose everything." There is also reference to "the foster-daughter of sixteen, sustained by daydreams and expectations" (i.e., Dina). The play at this stage was to be "a comedy," presumably of the same genre as *The League of Youth*.

In his next notes, made five years later, we find much more of the play as we know it. A scenic synopsis includes the schoolmaster reading to the assembled wives, the husbands discussing the railway, the foster-daughter (here called Valborg) impatient and longing to get away (to her mother, who is still alive), and Lona's arrival with the steamer; Act 1 ends with her "appearing in the doorway to the garden as the curtain falls." In Act 2, "the returned wanderers [i.e., Lona and the Captain] start turning things upside-down in the town. Rumours about the Captain's great wealth and the earlier scandal concerning Valborg's mother. The schoolmaster begins to think of getting engaged to Valborg. Conflict begins between the factory-owner and the Captain." Act 3: "News about irregularities in the repairs to the ship. The engagement is announced and celebrated. The Captain decides to leave the country. Fresh information from the yards. The factory-owner hesitates; for the moment, nothing must be said." Act 4: "Secret understanding between the Captain and Valborg. The railway project secured. Great ovations. Olaf runs away with the Captain and Valborg. Exciting final catastrophe."

The list of characters has by now grown considerably.

Apart from Bennick [*sic*], his wife, his blind mother and his sister Margrete (Martha), Miss "Hassel," the schoolmaster "Roerstad," Valborg (who suddenly becomes Dina), and Captain John Tennyson (later Rawlinson), we also have Madame Dorf, young Mrs Bernick's father Mads Toennesen (a "shipowner and master builder nicknamed 'The Badger' "), his other son Emil (altered to Hilmar), and Evensen, "a supply teacher." As synopsis follows synopsis, the list of characters changes; Aune, Sandstad and "Knap" appear, Bennick becomes Bernick, and the whole of the older generation is removed—Bernick's mother, Madame Dorf, Evensen the supply teacher and, eventually, Mads Toennesen, though he was to reappear three plays later as Morten Kiil in *An Enemy of the People*.

The drafts which follow comprise four versions of Act 1 or part of it, a draft of the whole play, and Ibsen's final fair copy in the version familiar to us. The first draft of Act 1 is different from the final version in numerous respects, and makes interesting reading. Among other things it contains a rare example of Ibsen trying to write English. The clerk Knap announces in Norwegian that since "the Captain fell overboard in the North Sea and the mate has delirium tremens," the *Indian Girl* has arrived under the command of "a sailor who was on board as a passenger . . . John Rawlinson, Esqr., New Orleans." Captain Rawlinson then appears and the following lively exchange takes place in English:

BERNICK: Good morning, master Rawlinson! This way, if you please, sir! I am master Bernick!

CAPTAIN RAWLINSON (*waves his handkerchief and cries*): Very well, Karsten; but first three hurrah for the old *grævling*![1]

The draft makes very spirited reading, and it is only when we compare it with the final version that we realize how much Ibsen gained in the rewriting. Bernick has much superfluous talk trimmed down, Lona is given a far more effective entrance, Aune (the only sympathetic portrait of a working-class man Ibsen ever attempted) is introduced quickly instead

[1] The Norwegian word for badger.

of having to wait until Act 2, a good deal of argument as to the pros and cons of the railway is cut, and we are told far more about the characters' past, notably Lona's quarrel with Bernick and the returned brother's supposed intrigue with Madame Dorf. Hilmar (who with his hypochondria and fanciful speech anticipates Hjalmar Ekdal in *The Wild Duck*) and Lona are much more sharply characterized; and the "floating coffin" issue, absent from the first draft, is introduced. The subsequent drafts show Ibsen groping painfully towards his final conception, and together they chart his progress from the vigorous but rather artless method of *The League of Youth* towards the compactness and inevitability of *A Doll's House*.

The Pillars of Society was not the first realistic prose play. Apart from *The League of Youth*, Bjoernson's two plays *A Bankrupt* and *The Editor*, both written in 1875, were explorations in this field. But these are not plays in the truest sense; they are melodramas which indict individual figures. *The Pillars of Society* was the first play to combine the three elements of colloquial dialogue, objectivity, and tightness of plot which are the requirements and characteristics of modern prose drama. The effect of the play on the younger generation of its time has been recorded by Otto Brahm, one of the founders of the Freie Buhne in Berlin, a theatre comparable in influence to Antoine's Théâtre Libre and Stanislavsky's Moscow Arts. In 1878, when Brahm was twenty-two, he saw *The Pillars of Society* at a small theatre in Berlin. Many years later he recalled that this was "the first strong theatrical impression" that he received. "It was," he said, "my first intimation of a new world of creative art."

MICHAEL MEYER

CHARACTERS

KARSTEN BERNICK	shipowner and consul
BETTY	his wife
OLAF	their son, aged thirteen
MARTHA	Karsten's sister
JOHAN TOENNESEN	Betty's younger brother
LONA HESSEL	her elder half-sister
HILMAR TOENNESEN	Betty's cousin
DR ROERLUND	a schoolmaster
MR RUMMEL	a wholesale dealer
MR VIGELAND	a merchant
MR SANDSTAD	a merchant
DINA DORF	a young girl living with the Bernicks
KRAP	a chief clerk
AUNE	a shipyard foreman
MRS RUMMEL	
MRS HOLT	the postmaster's wife
MRS LYNGE	wife of the local doctor
MISS RUMMEL	
MISS HOLT	

Townspeople and other residents, foreign seamen, steamship passengers, etc.

The action takes place in KARSTEN BERNICK'S house in a small Norwegian seaport.

ACT ONE

A spacious garden room in KARSTEN BERNICK'S *house. Down-stage left, a door leading to* BERNICK'S *room; upstage in the same wall is a similar door. In the centre of the opposite wall is a large entrance door. The rear wall is composed almost entirely of fine, clear glass, with an open door giving on to a broad verandah over which an awning is stretched. Steps lead down from the verandah into the garden, part of which can be seen, enclosed by a fence with a small gate. Beyond the fence is a street, the far side of which is lined with small wooden houses painted in bright colours. It is summer and the sun is shining warmly. Now and then people wander along the street; they stop and speak to each other, buy things from a little corner shop, etc.*

In the garden room a group of ladies is seated round a table. At the head of it sits MRS BERNICK; *on her left,* MRS HOLT *and her daughter; beyond them,* MRS RUMMEL *and* MISS RUMMEL. *On* MRS BERNICK'S *right sit* MRS LYNGE, MARTHA BERNICK *and* DINA DORF. *All the ladies are busy sewing. On the table lie large heaps of linen cut into shapes and half-finished, and other articles of clothing. Further upstage, at a little table on which stand two potted plants and a glass of lemonade,* DR ROERLUND, *the school-master, sits reading aloud from a book with gilt edges, though only the odd word can be heard by the audience. Outside in the garden,* OLAF BERNICK *is running about, shooting at a target with a bow and arrow.*

After a few moments, AUNE, *a shipyard foreman, enters quietly through the door on the right. The reading is interrupted briefly;* MRS BERNICK *nods to* AUNE *and points to the door on the left.* AUNE *walks quietly over and knocks softly on* BERNICK'S *door. Pause. He knocks again.* KRAP, *the chief clerk, comes out of the room with his hat in his hand and papers under his arm.*

KRAP: Oh, it's you?

AUNE: Mr Bernick sent for me.

KRAP: I know: but he can't see you himself. He's deputed me to tell you—

AUNE: You? I'd much rather speak to—

KRAP: He's deputed me to tell you this. You're to stop giving these talks to the men on Saturday evenings.

AUNE: Oh? I thought my free time was my own—

KRAP: You don't get free time in order for you to stop the men working. Last Saturday you told them their interests were threatened by the new machines and these new methods we've introduced down at the yard. Why d'you do it?

AUNE: For the good of the community.

KRAP: That's odd. Mr Bernick says this kind of thing will disintegrate the community.

AUNE: I don't mean by community what Mr Bernick does, Mr Krap. As foreman of the Workers' Association I—

KRAP: You're Mr Bernick's foreman. And the only community to which you owe allegiance is the Bernick Shipbuilding Company. That's where we all get our living. Well, now you know what Mr Bernick had to say to you.

AUNE: Mr Bernick wouldn't have said it like that, Mr Krap. But I know whom I've to thank for this. It's that damned American ship that's put in for repairs. Those people expect us to work like they do over there, and it isn't—

KRAP: Yes, well I haven't time to go into all that. Now you've heard Mr Bernick's orders, so stop this nonsense. Run back to the yard, now. I'm sure they need you there. I'll be down myself shortly. Pardon me, ladies!

He bows and goes out through the garden and down the street. AUNE exits quietly, right. DR ROERLUND, who has continued his reading during the foregoing dialogue, which has been conducted in subdued voices, finishes his book and closes it with a snap.

ROERLUND: And that, dear ladies, concludes our story.

MRS RUMMEL: Oh, what an instructive book!

MRS HOLT: And so moral!

MRS BERNICK: Yes, a book like that certainly gives one food for thought.

ROERLUND: Indeed, yes. It provides a salutary contrast to the horrors that confront us daily in the newspapers and magazines. This rouged and gilded exterior which Society flaunts before our eyes—what does it really hide? Hollowness and corruption—if I may use such words. No solid moral foundation. These so-called great modern communities are nothing but whited sepulchres.

MRS HOLT: How true!

MRS RUMMEL: We only need look at the crew of that American ship that's in port.

ROERLUND: I would rather not sully your ears by speaking of such human refuse. But even in respectable circles, what do we see? Doubt and unrest fermenting on every side; spiritual dissension and universal uncertainty. Out there, family life is everywhere undermined. An impudent spirit of subversion challenges our most sacred principles.

DINA (*without looking up*): But hasn't there been great progress too?

ROERLUND: Progress? I don't understand—

MRS HOLT (*amazed*): Dina, really!

MRS RUMMEL (*simultaneously*): Dina, how can you?

ROERLUND: I hardly think it would be healthy if this progress you speak of were to gain favour in our community. No; we in this little town should thank God that we are as we are. The occasional tare is, alas, to be found among the wheat here as elsewhere; but we strive with all the might that God has given us to root it up. We must keep our community pure, ladies. We must hold these untried theories which an impatient age would force upon us at arm's length.

MRS HOLT: Yes, there are many too many of them about.

MRS RUMMEL: Yes, last year we were only saved from having that horrible railway forced upon us by the skin of our teeth.

MRS BERNICK: Karsten put a stop to that.

ROERLUND: Providence, Mrs Bernick, Providence. You may rest assured that in refusing to countenance the scheme your husband was but the instrument of a Higher Purpose.

MRS BERNICK: But the way they attacked him in the newspapers! Oh, but dear Dr Roerlund, we've completely forgotten to thank you. It really is more than kind of you to sacrifice so much of your time for us.

ROERLUND: Oh, nonsense. My school has its holidays.

MRS BERNICK: Well, yes, but it's still a sacrifice, Dr Roerlund.

ROERLUND (*moves his chair closer*): Pray do not speak of it, dear lady. Are you not all making sacrifices for a noble cause? And do you not make them gladly and willingly? These depraved sinners whose moral condition we are striving to ameliorate are as wounded soldiers upon a battlefield; and you, dear ladies, are the Sisters of Mercy, the ministering angels who pick lint for these fallen creatures, wind your bandages gently round their wounds, tend and heal them—

MRS BERNICK: How wonderful to be able to view everything in such a charitable light.

ROERLUND: It is a gift one is born with; but much can be done to foster it. It is merely a question of having a serious vocation in life and viewing everything in the light of that vocation. What do you say, Miss Bernick? Do you not find that life has a more solid moral foundation since you decided to devote yourself to the noble task of educating the young?

MARTHA: I don't really know what to say. Sometimes as I sit there in the schoolroom I wish I were far away, on the wild sea.

ROERLUND: Temptation, my dear Miss Bernick! You must bar the door against such unruly guests. The wild sea—well, of course you don't mean that literally; you are thinking of the turbulent ocean of modern society in which so many human souls founder. Do you really envy that life you hear murmuring, nay, thundering outside? Only look down into the street. People walk there in the sunshine sweating and wrestling with their petty problems. No, we are better off who sit coolly here behind our windows with our backs turned on the direction from which unrest and disturbance might come.

MARTHA: Yes, of course. I'm sure you're right—

ROERLUND: And in a house such as this—a good, clean home,

where family life may be seen in its fairest form—where peace and harmony reign— (*To* MRS BERNICK) Are you listening for something, Mrs Bernick?

MRS BERNICK (*has turned towards the door downstage left*): How loudly they're talking in there!

ROERLUND: Is something important being discussed?

MRS BERNICK: I don't know. My husband seems to have someone with him.

HILMAR TOENNESEN, *with a cigar in his mouth, enters through the door on the right, but stops when he sees the ladies.*

HILMAR: Oh, I beg your pardon— (*Turns to leave*)

MRS BERNICK: No, come in, Hilmar; you're not disturbing us. Did you want something?

HILMAR: No, I was just looking in. Good morning, ladies. (*To* MRS BERNICK) Well, what's going to be the outcome?

MRS BERNICK: How do you mean?

HILMAR: Your husband's called a council of war.

MRS BERNICK: Oh? But what on earth about?

HILMAR: Oh, it's some nonsense about that confounded railway again.

MRS RUMMEL: How disgraceful!

MRS BERNICK: Poor Karsten! As if he hadn't enough worries already!

ROERLUND: But how is this possible, Mr Toennesen? Mr Bernick made it perfectly clear last year that he wouldn't have anything to with any railway.

HILMAR: Yes, that's what I thought. But I met Krap just now, and he tells me that the question's being reconsidered, and that Bernick's having a meeting with three of the other local plutocrats.

MRS RUMMEL: Yes, I thought I heard my husband's voice.

HILMAR: Oh yes, Rummel's there all right; and Sandstad who owns that big store up the hill; and Michael Vigeland—you know, the one they call Holy Mick—

ROERLUND *coughs.*

Oh, sorry, Doctor.

25

MRS BERNICK: Just when everything was so nice and peaceful here.

HILMAR: Well, personally I shouldn't be sorry if they started squabbling again. Give us a bit of fun—

ROERLUND: I think we can do without that kind of fun.

HILMAR: Depends on your temperament. Certain natures need to be harrowed by conflict occasionally. Provincial life doesn't provide many opportunities, worse luck; and not everybody has the guts to—(*Glances at* ROERLUND'S *book*) *Woman as the Servant of Society*. What's this rubbish?

MRS BERNICK: Good heavens, Hilmar, you mustn't say that! You can't have read it.

HILMAR: No, and I don't intend to.

MRS BERNICK: You don't seem in a very good temper today.

HILMAR: I'm not.

MRS BERNICK: Didn't you sleep well last night?

HILMAR: No, I slept rottenly. I took a walk yesterday evening —for my health, you know—and wandered into the Club and read a book some chap had written about the North Pole. I find it very good for my nerves to read about man's struggle with the elements.

MRS RUMMEL: It doesn't appear to have agreed with you, Mr Toennesen.

HILMAR: No, it didn't really agree with me. I tossed and turned all night. Dreamed I was being chased by a horrible walrus.

OLAF (*who has come up on to the verandah*): Have you been chased by a walrus, Uncle?

HILMAR: I dreamed it, you young jackass. Are you still playing with that silly bow? Why don't you get yourself a proper rifle?

OLAF: Oh, I'd love one! But—

HILMAR: There's some sense in having a rifle. That slow pressure on the trigger, you know—good for the nerves.

OLAF: And I could shoot bears with it, Uncle! But Father won't let me.

MRS BERNICK: You mustn't put such ideas into his head, Hilmar.

26

HILMAR: Hm! Fine lot his generation's going to be! All this talk about the importance of sport, and all they do is play silly games, when they ought to be toughening their characters by staring danger unflinchingly in the face. Don't stand there pointing that bow at me, you little fool, it might go off.

OLAF: But Uncle, there's no arrow in it.

HILMAR: You can never be sure. There might be. Point it somewhere else, I tell you. Why the devil don't you go over to America on one of your father's ships? You could hunt buffaloes there. Or fight redskins.

MRS BERNICK: Hilmar, really!

OLAF: Oh yes, Uncle, I'd love to! And I might meet Uncle Johan and Aunt Lona!

HILMAR: Hm—I shouldn't bother about that.

MRS BERNICK: You can go back into the garden now, Olaf.

OLAF: Can I go out into the street too, Mother?

MRS BERNICK: Yes, but not too far.

OLAF runs out through the garden gate.

ROERLUND: You ought not to stuff the child's head with such ideas, Mr Toennesen.

HILMAR: Oh, no. Of course not. He's got to spend the rest of his life sitting safe at home, like all the others.

ROERLUND: Why don't you go to America yourself?

HILMAR: I? In my state of health? But of course no one in this town bothers about that. Besides, one has certain responsibilities towards the community one lives in. There's got to be someone here to keep the flag of ideals flying. Ugh, now he's started shouting again.

LADIES: Who? Shouting? Who is shouting?

HILMAR: I don't know. They're raising their voices in there, and it's very bad for my nerves.

MRS RUMMEL: Ah, that's my husband, Mr Toennesen. He's so used to addressing public meetings.

ROERLUND: The others aren't doing too badly either, by the sound of it.

HILMAR: But of course! The moment their pockets are threatened— Oh, everyone here's so petty and materialistic. Ugh!

27

Mrs Bernick: Well anyway, that's better than the old days, when people thought of nothing but dissipation.

Mrs Lynge: Were things really so dreadful here before?

Mrs Rummel: Indeed they were, Mrs Lynge. You may think yourself fortunate that you didn't live here then.

Mrs Holt: Yes, there have certainly been great changes. When I think of what things were like when I was a young girl—

Mrs Rummel: Oh, you only need to look back fifteen years. My word, the goings on there used to be! Why, there was a dance club, *and* a musical society—

Martha: And a dramatic society. I remember that well.

Mrs Rummel: Yes, it was they who put on that play of yours, Mr Toennesen.

Hilmar (*upstage*): Really? Oh, I don't—er—

Roerlund: Mr Toennesen wrote a play?

Mrs Rummel: Why, yes. Long before you came here, Dr Roerlund. It only ran for one night.

Mrs Lynge: Wasn't that the play you were telling me about in which you acted one of the young lovers, Mrs Rummel?

Mrs Rummel (*shoots a glance at* Roerlund): I? I really don't recall that, Mrs Lynge. But I do remember all the dreadful parties that used to go on.

Mrs Holt: Yes, I know houses where they used to hold big parties twice a week.

Mrs Lynge: And I hear there was a company of strolling players that used to come here.

Mrs Rummel: Yes, they were the worst of all—

Mrs Holt *coughs uneasily*.

Er—strolling players, did you say? No, I don't remember them.

Mrs Lynge: But I hear they got up to all kinds of wicked pranks. Tell me, is there any truth in those stories?

Mrs Rummel: None whatever, Mrs Lynge, I assure you.

Mrs Holt: Dina, my love, pass me that piece of linen, will you?

Mrs Bernick (*simultaneously*): Dina dear, run out and ask Katrine to bring us some coffee.

Martha: I'll come with you, Dina.

28

DINA *and* MARTHA *go out through the door upstage left.*

MRS BERNICK: If you'll excuse me for a moment, ladies, I think we'll take coffee outside.

She goes out on to the verandah and lays a table. DR ROERLUND *stands in the doorway talking to her.* HILMAR TOENNESEN *sits down outside and smokes.*

MRS RUMMEL (*quietly*): My goodness, Mrs Lynge, how you frightened me!

MRS LYNGE: I?

MRS HOLT: Yes, but you started it really, Mrs Rummel.

MRS RUMMEL: I? How can you say such a thing, Mrs Holt? I never let a single word pass my lips.

MRS LYNGE: But what is all this?

MRS RUMMEL: How could you bring up the subject of—! I mean, really! Didn't you see Dina was here?

MRS LYNGE: Dina? But good heavens, is there anything the matter with—?

MRS HOLT: And in this house? Don't you know it was Mrs Bernick's brother who—?

MRS LYNGE: What about him? I don't know anything—I'm a newcomer here—

MRS RUMMEL: You mean you haven't heard about—? Hm. (*To* MISS RUMMEL) Hilda dear, run down into the garden for a few minutes.

MRS HOLT: You too, Netta. And be sure you're nice to poor dear Dina when she comes back.

MISS RUMMEL *and* MISS HOLT *go into the garden.*

MRS LYNGE: Well? What was this about Mrs Bernick's brother?

MRS RUMMEL: Don't you know it was he who was involved in that dreadful scandal?

MRS LYNGE: Mr Toennesen was involved in a dreadful scandal?

MRS RUMMEL: Oh good heavens no, Mr Toennesen is her cousin, Mrs Lynge. I'm talking about her brother—

MRS HOLT: The Prodigal of the family—

MRS RUMMEL: His name was Johan. He ran away to America.

Mrs Holt: Had to, you understand.

Mrs Lynge: And it was he who was involved in this dreadful scandal?

Mrs Rummel: Yes. It was a kind of a—what shall I call it?—a kind of a—with Dina's mother. Oh, I remember it as if it had happened yesterday. Johan Toennesen was working in old Mrs Bernick's office. Karsten Bernick had just come back from Paris—he hadn't got engaged yet—

Mrs Lynge: Yes, but the dreadful scandal?

Mrs Rummel: Well, you see, that winter a theatrical troupe was here in town—

Mrs Holt: And among them was an actor named Dorf, and his wife. All the young men were quite crazy about her.

Mrs Rummel: Yes, heaven knows what they could see in her. Well, Mr Dorf came home late one night—

Mrs Holt: Unexpectedly, you understand—

Mrs Rummel: And what should he find but—no, I really can't bring myself to speak of it.

Mrs Holt: No, Mrs Rummel, he didn't *find* anything. The door was locked. From the inside.

Mrs Rummel: Yes, well, that's what I'm saying—he found the door locked. And, would you believe it, he—the man who was inside—had to jump out of the window!

Mrs Holt: Right out of one of the top windows!

Mrs Lynge: And the man was Mrs Bernick's brother?

Mrs Rummel: It was indeed.

Mrs Lynge: And that was why he ran away to America?

Mrs Holt: Yes. Well, of course he had to.

Mrs Rummel: And then afterwards they discovered something almost equally dreadful. Would you believe it, he'd stolen some of the firm's money!

Mrs Holt: But we don't know that for sure, Mrs Rummel. It may only have been gossip.

Mrs Rummel: Oh, but now, really! Didn't the whole town know about it? Didn't old Mrs Bernick practically go bankrupt because of it? My husband told me so himself. But Heaven forbid that *I* should say anything!

MRS HOLT: Well, anyway, Mrs Dorf didn't get the money because she—

MRS LYNGE: Yes, what happened between Dina's parents after that?

MRS RUMMEL: Well, Dorf went away and left his wife and child. But Madam had the cheek to stay here a whole year more. Of course, she didn't dare show her face at the theatre. She kept herself by taking in washing and sewing—

MRS HOLT: And tried to start a dancing academy.

MRS RUMMEL: Of course, nothing came of it. What parents would entrust their children to the care of a person like that? Besides, as things turned out she didn't last long. She wasn't used to hard work, not that fine lady. She picked up some chest trouble, and died.

MRS LYNGE: Well, that was a dreadful scandal indeed.

MRS RUMMEL: Yes, it's been a terrible cross for the Bernicks to bear. It's been the one skeleton in their cupboard, as my husband once phrased it. So don't ever mention the subject in this house, Mrs Lynge.

MRS HOLT: Or the half-sister, for heaven's sake!

MRS LYNGE: Mrs Bernick has a half-sister too?

MRS RUMMEL: Did have—fortunately. It's all over between them now. Oh, she was a queer one all right. Would you believe it, she cut her hair off, and when it rained she walked round in gumboots just like a man!

MRS HOLT: And when the half-brother—the Prodigal—ran away, and the whole town quite naturally raised a hue and cry against him, do you know what she did? Went over and joined him!

MRS RUMMEL: Yes, but the scandal she created before she went, Mrs Holt!

MRS HOLT: Hush, let's not talk of that.

MRS LYNGE: My goodness, was she involved in a scandal too?

MRS RUMMEL: Well, it was like this. Karsten Bernick had just got engaged to Betty Toennesen; and he was going in to announce the news to her aunt, with his newly-betrothed on his arm—

31

MRS HOLT: The Toennesens had lost their parents, you see—

MRS RUMMEL: —when Lona Hessel got up from the chair she was sitting on and gave Karsten Bernick for all his fine airs and breeding such a box on the ears she nearly split his eardrums.

MRS LYNGE: You don't mean it!

MRS RUMMEL: As heaven is my witness.

MRS HOLT: And packed her bags and went to America.

MRS LYNGE: Then she must have had her eye on him too!

MRS RUMMEL: Of course she had! She'd been flouncing round here imagining that he'd marry her the moment he got back from Paris.

MRS HOLT: Yes, fancy her being able to believe that! A man of the world like Karsten Bernick—so genteel and well-bred—the perfect gentleman—every woman's dream—

MRS RUMMEL: And so virtuous with it all, Mrs Holt. So moral.

MRS LYNGE: But what has this Miss Hessel been doing in America?

MRS RUMMEL: Ah. Over that hangs a veil which had best not be lifted, as my husband once phrased it.

MRS LYNGE: What do you mean?

MRS RUMMEL: Well, the family's no longer in contact with her, as you can imagine. But the whole town knows this much, that she's sung for money over there in—hm—places of entertainment—

MRS HOLT: And given lectures in public—

MRS RUMMEL: And brought out a wicked book.

MRS LYNGE: My goodness!

MRS RUMMEL: Yes, Lona Hessel is another skeleton in the Bernick family cupboard. Well, now you know the whole story, Mrs Lynge. Of course I've only told you all this so that you'll be on your guard.

MRS LYNGE: My goodness yes, you can be sure I will. But that poor Dina Dorf! I feel really sorry for her.

MRS RUMMEL: Oh, it was a great stroke of luck as far as she was concerned. Just imagine if she'd been left in the hands of those parents of hers! We all lent her a helping hand, of course, and did what we could to try to guide her along the right paths. Then Miss Bernick arranged for her to come and live here.

MRS HOLT: But she's always been a difficult child. Well, what can you expect, when you think of the example she's been set? A girl like that isn't like one of us. We have to take her as we find her, Mrs Lynge.

MRS RUMMEL: Hush, here she is. (*Loudly*) Yes, dear Dina's a very clever girl. Oh, hullo, Dina, are you back? We're just finishing.

MRS HOLT: Dina, my sweet, how lovely your coffee smells. There's nothing like a nice cup of morning coffee—

MRS BERNICK (*outside on the verandah*): Everything is ready, ladies!

MISS BERNICK *and* DINA *have meanwhile been helping the* MAID *to bring in the coffee things. All the* LADIES *go out on to the verandah and sit down. They talk to* DINA *with ostentatious amiability. After a few moments, she comes into the room and looks for her sewing.*

MRS BERNICK (*outside at the coffee table*): Dina, won't you join us?

DINA: No, thank you. I don't want any.

She sits down to her sewing. MRS BERNICK *and* DR ROERLUND *exchange a few words; then he comes into the room.*

ROERLUND (*pretends to need something from the table; then says softly*): Dina.

DINA: Yes.

ROERLUND: Why don't you want to sit outside with us?

DINA: When I came in with the coffee I could see from the expression on that new lady's face that they'd been talking about me.

ROERLUND: But didn't you also notice how friendly she was to you on the verandah?

DINA: That's just what I can't bear.

ROERLUND: You have a stubborn nature, Dina.

DINA: Yes.

ROERLUND: Why?

DINA: That's the way I am.

ROERLUND: Couldn't you try to make yourself different?

DINA: No.

ROERLUND: Why not?

DINA (*looks at him*): I'm one of the depraved sinners.

ROERLUND: Dina!

DINA: Mother was a depraved sinner too.

ROERLUND: Who has told you about these things?

DINA: No one. They never tell me anything. Why don't they? They all treat me so gently, as though I might break into pieces if— Oh, how I hate all this kindness!

ROERLUND: Dina dear, I understand so well how confined you feel here, but—

DINA: Yes, if only I could go far away. I'm sure I could manage on my own if only I didn't live among people who were so—so—

ROERLUND: So what?

DINA: So virtuous and moral.

ROERLUND: Dina, you can't mean that.

DINA: Oh, you know what I mean. Every day Hilda and Netta are brought here so that I can model myself on them. I can never be as clever as them. I don't want to be. Oh, if only I were far away! Then I might be able to become someone.

ROERLUND: You are someone, Dina.

DINA: What's the use, here?

ROERLUND: Then you mean you're seriously thinking of going away?

DINA: I wouldn't stay a day longer, if you weren't here.

ROERLUND: Tell me, Dina. Why do you like being with me?

DINA: Because you teach me so much about what's beautiful.

ROERLUND: I teach you about what is beautiful?

DINA: Yes. Or rather—you don't teach me anything; but when I hear you talk, I understand what beauty is.

ROERLUND: What do you mean by beauty?

DINA: I've never thought.

ROERLUND: Well, think now. What do you mean by beauty?

DINA: Beauty—is something that is big—and far away.

ROERLUND: Hm. Dina my dear, I'm deeply concerned about you.

34

DINA: Is that all?

ROERLUND: You know how very dear you are to me.

DINA: If I were Hilda or Netta you wouldn't be afraid to let people see it.

ROERLUND: Oh, Dina, you don't understand all the little things a man has to— When a man is chosen to be a moral pillar for the society he lives in—well, he can't be sufficiently careful. If only I could be sure that people would not misinterpret my motives—! Well, it can't be helped. You must and shall be rescued. Dina, is it a bargain that when I come—when circumstances permit me to come to you and say: "Here is my hand"—you will take it and be my wife? Will you promise me that, Dina?

DINA: Yes.

ROERLUND: Thank you—thank you! Because I, too—oh, Dina, you are so very dear to me. Hush, someone's coming! Dina —please—for my sake—go outside and join the others.

She goes out and joins the LADIES. *As she does so* MR RUMMEL, MR SANDSTAD *and* MR VIGELAND *enter from the room downstage left, followed by* MR BERNICK, *with a sheaf of papers in his hand.*

BERNICK: Right, then, we're agreed.

VIGELAND: Yes, yes. May God's blessing rest upon our plans!

RUMMEL: Never you fear, Bernick. A Norseman's word is his bond. You know that.

BERNICK: There's to be no going back, now. No one's to drop out, whatever opposition we may encounter.

RUMMEL: We stand or fall together, Bernick.

HILMAR (*who has come to the door of the verandah*): Fall? What's going to fall? Railway shares?

BERNICK: On the contrary. The railway is to go ahead.

RUMMEL: Full steam, Mr Toennesen.

HILMAR (*comes closer*): Really?

ROERLUND: What?

MRS BERNICK (*at the verandah door*): But Karsten dear, surely you—?

BERNICK: Betty dear, how can these things possibly interest

35

you? (*To the* THREE GENTLEMEN) Well, we must get out a prospectus as quickly as possible. Our names will head the list, of course. The positions we occupy in the community render it our duty to support this cause to the fullest limit of our generosity.

SANDSTAD: Of course, of course.

RUMMEL: We'll see it through, Bernick. You have our word.

BERNICK: Oh yes, I'm not worried about the outcome. But we must use our authority and influence; once we can show that every section of the community is actively participating, the municipality will feel compelled to subscribe its share.

MRS BERNICK: Karsten, you must come outside and tell us all about it.

BERNICK: My dear Betty, this is not a matter for women to concern themselves with.

HILMAR: You seriously mean you're letting this railway project go through after all?

BERNICK: Yes, of course.

ROERLUND: But Mr Bernick, last year you—

BERNICK: Last year the situation was different. The plan then was for a line to run along the coast—

VIGELAND: Which would have been utterly superfluous, Dr Roerlund. After all, we have ships—

SANDSTAD: And it'd have been prohibitively expensive—

RUMMEL: Yes, and would have damaged important interests in our town.

BERNICK: The main point is that the project as then conceived would not have benefited the community as a whole. That is why I opposed it; and as a result, they have decided to run the line inland.

HILMAR: Yes, but then it won't touch any of the towns round here.

BERNICK: It will touch our town, my dear Hilmar. We have arranged for a branch line to be built.

HILMAR: Oh? That's a new idea, isn't it?

RUMMEL: Yes—magnificent idea, isn't it? What?

ROERLUND: Hm.

VIGELAND: There's no denying that Providence might almost

36

have designed that little valley especially so as to accommodate a branch line.

ROERLUND: Do you really think so, Mr Vigeland?

BERNICK: Yes, I must confess that I, too, feel it was the hand of Providence that sent me up-country on business last spring and directed my footsteps into this valley, which I had never seen before. Suddenly it struck me like an inspiration that through this valley we could lay a branch line to our little town. I arranged for an engineer to survey the land and I have here his provisional calculations and estimates. Nothing now stands in our way.

MRS BERNICK (*still in the doorway, with the other* LADIES): But Karsten dear, why have you kept all this hidden from us?

BERNICK: My dear Betty, you wouldn't have been able to understand what it was all about. In any case I haven't mentioned it to anyone until today. But now the decisive moment has arrived. Now we can work openly and with all our strength. Yes, I shall force this project through, even if it means staking everything I possess.

RUMMEL: Us too, Bernick. You can rely on us.

ROERLUND: You really expect so much from this project then, gentlemen?

BERNICK: Of course we do! Think what a stimulus it will give to our whole community! Think of the great tracts of forest it will render accessible! Think of the mines it will enable us to work! Think of the river with its waterfalls one above the other, and the factories we could build to utilize their power! A whole wealth of new industries will spring into being!

ROERLUND: But are you not afraid of the possible consequences of more frequent contact with the depraved world outside?

BERNICK: No need to fear that, my dear Doctor. Nowadays our industrious little community rests, thank God, on a sound moral foundation. We have all, if I may say so, helped to cleanse it; and we shall continue to keep it clean, each in his own way. You, Dr Roerlund, will maintain your splendid work at the school and in the home. We, the practical men of affairs, will strengthen the community by spreading prosperity over as broad a circle as possible. And our womenfolk—yes, ladies, come closer, you may listen to what I have to say—our womenfolk, I say, our wives and daughters—continue, ladies, I beseech you, to labour untiringly in the cause of charity, and to be a help and a shield to your dear ones, as my beloved Betty and Martha are to me and to Olaf— (*Looks round*) Yes, where is Olaf today?

MRS BERNICK: Oh, now the holidays have begun it's hopeless to try to keep him indoors.

BERNICK: I suppose that means he's down on the waterfront again. He'll have an accident before he's finished, you mark my word.

HILMAR: Oh, rubbish. A little skirmish with the elements—

MRS RUMMEL: Oh, I think it's so wonderful the love you show your family, Mr Bernick.

BERNICK: Well, the family is the basis on which society rests. A good home, loyal and trustworthy friends, a small close-knit circle with no intrusive elements to cast their shadow—

KRAP *enters right with letters and newspapers.*

KRAP: The foreign mail, Mr Bernick. And a telegram from New York.

BERNICK (*takes it*): Ah, this'll be from the owners of the *Indian Girl.*

RUMMEL: Has the post come? Then I must ask you to excuse me—

VIGELAND: Me too.

SANDSTAD: Goodbye, Mr Bernick.

BERNICK: Goodbye, gentlemen, goodbye. And don't forget, we meet at five o'clock this afternoon.

THE THREE GENTLEMEN: Yes, yes. Of course.

They go out right.

BERNICK (*reads the telegram*): Oh no, really, this is typically American! How absolutely disgraceful!

MRS BERNICK: Oh, Karsten, what is it?

BERNICK: Look at this, Mr Krap. Here, read it.

KRAP (*reads*): "Execute minimum repairs. Despatch *Indian Girl* as soon as seaworthy. Safe season. At worst, cargo will keep her afloat." Well, bless my soul!

BERNICK: "Cargo will keep her afloat"! Those fellows know perfectly well that if anything goes wrong that cargo'll send the ship to the bottom like a stone.

ROERLUND: Well, that only goes to show what the moral climate is like in these so-called great communities.

BERNICK: You're right. They don't even respect human life, as long as they make their profit. (*To* KRAP) Can we make the *Indian Girl* seaworthy in four or five days?

KRAP: Yes, if Mr Vigeland lets us stop work on the *Palm Tree*.

BERNICK: Hm. He won't do that. Well, look through the mail. By the way, did you see Olaf down on the jetty?

KRAP: No, sir.

He goes into the room downstage left.

BERNICK (*reads the telegram again*): Eighteen human lives at stake! And those gentlemen don't turn a hair.

HILMAR: Well, it's a sailor's job to brave the elements. It must be exhilarating to have nothing but a thin plank between yourself and eternity. Good for the nerves—

BERNICK: I'd like to meet the shipowner in this town who could reconcile his conscience to giving an order like this. There isn't a man in this community, not one— (*Sees* OLAF) Ah, here he is. Thank goodness for that.

OLAF, *with a fishing-line in his hand, has run up the street and in through the garden gate.*

OLAF (*still in the garden*): Uncle Hilmar, I've been down looking at the steamer!

BERNICK: Have you been on that jetty again?

OLAF: No, I only went out in a boat. Just fancy, Uncle Hilmar, a whole circus has come ashore, with horses and animals! And there were lots of tourists too!

MRS RUMMEL: I say, are we going to see a circus?

ROERLUND: We? I hardly think so.

MRS RUMMEL: No, no—of course, I didn't mean *us*—I only—

DINA: I should like to see a circus.

OLAF: Yes, so would I!

HILMAR: You little fool, what's worth seeing there? *Dressage*, and all that nonsense. Now, to see a gaucho galloping across the pampas on his snorting mustang—that'd be different! Oh dear, these provincial backwaters—

OLAF (*tugs* MARTHA'S *sleeve*): Look, Aunt Martha, look! There they are!

MRS HOLT: Oh, my goodness!

MRS LYNGE: Dear me, what horrible people.

A crowd of TOURISTS *and* TOWNSPEOPLE *appears in the street.*

MRS RUMMEL: My word, they're proper vagabonds. Look at that woman in the grey dress, Mrs Holt. She's carrying a knapsack on her back!

MRS HOLT: Yes. Fancy, she's got it tied to her parasol! I expect she's the ringmaster's—er—wife.

MRS RUMMEL: There's the ringmaster! The one with the beard. I say, he looks just like a pirate! Don't look at him, Hilda.

MRS HOLT: Nor you, Netta.

OLAF: Mother, he's waving to us!

BERNICK: What!

MRS BERNICK: Olaf, what on earth do you mean?

MRS RUMMEL: My goodness, yes! The woman's waving too!

BERNICK: This really is intolerable.

MARTHA (*gives an involuntary cry*): Oh!

MRS BERNICK: What is it, Martha?

MARTHA: Oh, nothing. I thought for a moment it—

OLAF (*cries excitedly*): Look, look! Here come the horses and animals! And there are the Americans, too! All the sailors from the *Indian Girl!*

"Yankee Doodle" *is heard, accompanied by a clarinet and drum.*

HILMAR (*puts his hands over his ears*): Ugh, ugh, ugh!

ROERLUND: I think we should isolate ourselves for a while, ladies. This is not for us. Let us return to our work.

MRS BERNICK: Ought we perhaps to draw the curtains?
ROERLUND: That is exactly what I had in mind.

The LADIES *take their places again at the table.* DR ROERLUND *closes the verandah door and draws the curtains across it and the windows. The room is plunged into semi-darkness.*

OLAF (*peering out*): Mother, now the ringmaster's lady's washing her face at the pump.
MRS BERNICK: What! In the middle of the market-place?
HILMAR: Well, if I was crossing a desert and happened on a well, I don't suppose I'd bother to look round to see if— ugh, that dreadful clarinet!
ROERLUND: This is becoming a matter for the police.
BERNICK: Ah well, they're foreigners; one mustn't judge them too severely. These people are not born with the sense of decorum which makes us instinctively obey the laws of propriety. Let them go their way. What are they to us? This ribald behaviour, offensive to every standard of decency, fortunately has no place in our community. What the—!

The STRANGE LADY *strides in through the door, right.*

THE LADIES (*in terrified whispers*): The circus woman! The ringmaster's—er—!
MRS BERNICK: Good heavens! What is the meaning of this?
MARTHA (*jumps to her feet*): Oh!
THE LADY: Morning, Betty dear. Morning, Martha. Morning, brother-in-law.
MRS BERNICK (*with a scream*): Lona!
BERNICK (*takes a step backwards*): Good God!
MRS HOLT: Oh, dear heaven!
MRS RUMMEL: It can't be possible!
HILMAR: Well! Ugh!
MRS BERNICK: Lona! Is it really you!
MISS HESSEL: Really me? Sure it's me. Come on, kiss me and prove it!
HILMAR: Ugh! Ugh!
MRS BERNICK: You mean you've come here to—?
BERNICK: To perform?

41

MISS HESSEL: Perform? What do you mean, perform?

BERNICK: In the—er—circus.

MISS HESSEL (*roars with laughter*): Karsten, have you gone nuts? You think I've joined the circus? No—I've learned a few tricks, and acted the clown in more ways than one— (MRS RUMMEL *coughs*)—but I haven't started jumping through hoops yet.

BERNICK: Then you're not—!

MRS BERNICK: Thank heaven for that!

MISS HESSEL: No, we came respectably, with the other tourists. Steerage—but we're used to that.

MRS BERNICK: Did you say *we*?

BERNICK (*takes a step towards her*): Whom do you mean by *we*?

MISS HESSEL: Me and the kid, of course.

THE LADIES (*shriek*): Kid?

HILMAR: What!

ROERLUND: Well, really!

MRS BERNICK: But Lona, what do you mean?

MISS HESSEL: Who do you think I mean? John, of course; he's the only kid I have, to my knowledge. Johan, you used to call him.

MRS BERNICK: Johan!

MRS RUMMEL (sotto voce *to* MRS LYNGE): The Prodigal!

BERNICK (*unwillingly*): Is Johan with you?

MISS HESSEL: Yes, of course. Never go anywhere without him. Say, you *are* all looking down in the mouth. Why are you sitting in the dark? What's that white stuff you're all sewing? Is someone dead?

ROERLUND: Madam, you find yourself at a meeting of the Society for the Redemption of Fallen Women.

MISS HESSEL (*lowers her voice*): What! You mean all these respectable-looking ladies are—?

MRS RUMMEL: Now, really!

MISS HESSEL: Oh, I get it, I get it. Well, if it isn't Mrs Rummel! And Mrs Holt! Say, we three haven't grown any shorter in the tooth since we last met! Now, listen, all of you. Let the Fallen Women wait for twenty-four hours; they won't fall any further. This is an occasion for celebration!

ROERLUND: A homecoming is not always an occasion for celebration.

MISS HESSEL: Is that so? How do you interpret your Bible, Reverend—

ROERLUND: I am not a Reverend.

MISS HESSEL: Never mind, you'll become one. Say, this charity stuff stinks awful. Just like a shroud. Of course, I'm used to the prairies. Air's fresher there.

BERNICK (*mops his brow*): Yes, it is rather close in here.

MISS HESSEL: Take it easy, Karsten. You'll surface. (*Pulls aside the curtains*) Let's have some daylight in here for when the kid comes. Wait till you see him! He's scrubbed himself as clean as a—

HILMAR: Ugh!

MISS HESSEL (*opens the door and windows*): That's to say, he *will* have, once he gets a chance up at the hotel. On that ship he got as filthy as a pig.

HILMAR: Ugh! Ugh!

MISS HESSEL: Ugh? Well, bless me if it isn't—! (*Points at HILMAR and asks the others*) Does he still sit around here saying "Ugh!"?

HILMAR: I *don't* sit around I only stay here because my health doesn't permit me to work.

ROERLUND (*coughs*): Ladies, I hardly think—

MISS HESSEL (*catches sight of* OLAF): Is this yours, Betty? Give us your paw, kid. Are you afraid of your ugly old aunt?

ROERLUND (*puts his book under his arm*): Ladies, I hardly think the atmosphere here is conducive to further work today. We meet again as usual tomorrow?

MISS HESSEL (*as the other* LADIES *rise to leave*): Sure, why not? You can count me in.

ROERLUND: You? Forgive my asking, madam, but what can you possibly contribute to our Society?

MISS HESSEL: Fresh air—Reverend!

ACT TWO

The garden room in BERNICK'S *house.* MRS BERNICK *is seated alone at the work-table with her sewing. After a few moments,* BERNICK *enters right with his hat on, carrying gloves and a stick.*

MRS BERNICK: Home already, Karsten?

BERNICK: Yes. I have an appointment here.

MRS BERNICK (*sighs*): Oh, dear. Johan again, I suppose.

BERNICK: No, no, it's with one of the men. (*Takes off his hat*) Where are all the ladies today?

MRS BERNICK: Mrs Rummel and Hilda hadn't time.

BERNICK: Oh? They sent their excuses?

MRS BERNICK: Yes; they had so much to do at home.

BERNICK: But of course. And the others won't be coming either, I suppose?

MRS BERNICK: No, they're busy too.

BERNICK: I could have told you that yesterday. Where's Olaf?

MRS BERNICK: I sent him out for a walk with Dina.

BERNICK: Hm. Dina. Flighty young hussy. Striking up like that with Johan the very first day he arrived—

MRS BERNICK: But Karsten dear, Dina knows nothing about—

BERNICK: Well, he ought to have had the tact not to pay her so much attention. I saw the look Vigeland gave them.

MRS BERNICK (*puts her sewing in her lap*): Karsten, why do you think they've come?

BERNICK: Well, I dare say that farm of his isn't doing too well —she said yesterday they'd had to travel steerage—

MRS BERNICK: Yes, I'm afraid you must be right. But fancy *her* coming with him! After the dreadful way she insulted you!

BERNICK: Oh, that was a long time ago. Forget about it.

MRS BERNICK: How can I forget about it? After all, he is my

44

brother—but it's not so much him I'm thinking of as all the unpleasantness it's causing you. Oh, Karsten, I'm so dreadfully frightened—

BERNICK: Frightened? Of what?

MRS BERNICK: Mightn't they arrest him for stealing that money from your mother?

BERNICK: Don't be so silly. No one can prove anything was taken.

MRS BERNICK: Oh, but the whole town knows. And you've said yourself that—

BERNICK: I have said nothing. The town knows nothing. All they heard was just vague gossip.

MRS BERNICK: You are so magnanimous, Karsten.

BERNICK: Try to forget these old memories, Betty. You don't know how it distresses me to be reminded about all this. (*Walks up and down; then he throws down his stick*) Why on earth must they come home just at this moment, when I don't want any trouble in the town; or in the press? It'll get into every local paper for miles around. Whether I welcome them or whether I turn my back on them, people will talk about it and read something into it. They'll dig the whole story up again, just the way you're doing. And in a community like ours— (*Throws down his gloves on the table*) And I haven't a single person I can talk to or look to for support.

MRS BERNICK: Have you no one, Karsten?

BERNICK: No, who could there be? Oh, why in God's name must they come *now*? They're sure to create a scandal of some kind or another. Especially she. It really is intolerable having people like that in one's own family.

MRS BERNICK: Well, I can't help it if—

BERNICK: You can't help what? That they're your relations? No, you can't help that.

MRS BERNICK: I didn't ask them to come.

BERNICK: Oh, here we go again. "I didn't ask them to come. I didn't write and beg them. I didn't drag them here by the hair." I know it all by heart!

MRS BERNICK (*begins to cry*): Oh, why must you be so unkind?

45

BERNICK: That's right. Start crying, and give the town something else to talk about. Stop this foolishness, Betty. Go and sit outside, someone might come. Do you want people to see you've been crying? A fine thing it'd be if people got to hear that— hush, someone's coming.

There is a knock on the door.

Come in!

MRS BERNICK *goes out on to the verandah with her sewing.* AUNE *enters, right.*

AUNE: Good morning, Mr Bernick.

BERNICK: Good morning. Well, I suppose you can guess why I've sent for you?

AUNE: Mr Krap said something yesterday about your not being satisfied with—

BERNICK: I'm dissatisfied with the way things are going down at the yard, Aune. You're not getting on with those repairs. The *Palm Tree* ought to have been under sail days ago. Mr Vigeland comes here to complain every day. He's a difficult man to have as a partner.

AUNE: The *Palm Tree* can sail the day after tomorrow.

BERNICK: At last! But that American ship, the *Indian Girl*, has been lying here for five weeks—

AUNE: The American? I understood we were to put all our men on to your ship till she was ready.

BERNICK: I gave no such orders. My instructions were that you should go full steam ahead with the American too. You haven't.

AUNE: But her bottom's rotten, Mr Bernick. The more we patch her the worse she gets.

BERNICK: That's not the real reason. Mr Krap's told me the whole story. You don't understand how to use these new machines I've bought—or rather, you won't use them.

AUNE: Mr Bernick, I'm nearly sixty and ever since I was a boy I've been accustomed to the old methods—

BERNICK: We can't use those nowadays. Look, Aune, you mustn't think I'm doing this for money. Luckily I don't need any more of that. I've got to think of the community of which I'm a member, and of the business of which I am the head. Progress has got to come from me or it won't come at all.

AUNE: I want progress too, Mr Bernick.

BERNICK: Yes, for your own narrow circle, the working class. Oh, I know you agitators. You make speeches and get the people worked up, but the moment anyone takes any practical steps towards improving matters, as with these machines, you refuse to co-operate, and get frightened.

AUNE: I am frightened, Mr Bernick. I'm frightened for all the mouths from which these machines will take the bread. You keep on saying we've got to think of the community, but I reckon the community owes us a duty too. What's the use of society employing knowledge and capital to introduce all these new inventions before it's educated a generation that knows how to use them?

BERNICK: You read and think too much, Aune. And what good do you get from it? It just makes you discontented with your position in society.

AUNE: It isn't that, Mr Bernick. I can't bear to see one good man after another getting sacked and their families going hungry to make way for these machines.

BERNICK: When printing was invented, many scribes went hungry.

AUNE: Would you have welcomed it if you'd been a scribe?

BERNICK: I didn't send for you to argue with you. The *Indian Girl*'s got to be ready to sail the day after tomorrow.

AUNE: But, Mr Bernick—

BERNICK: The day after tomorrow, do you hear? At the same time as our own ship; not an hour later. I've good reasons for wanting to get the job done quickly. Have you read the newspaper this morning? Then you know that the Americans have been causing trouble again. Those ruffians are turning the whole town upside down; not a night goes by without them starting a brawl in the streets or in a drinking-house. To say nothing of other things I'd rather not mention.

AUNE: Yes, they seem a bad lot.

BERNICK: And who gets the blame for all this? I do! It all comes back on to my head. These newspaper fellows grumble and try to insinuate that we've put all our labour strength on to the *Palm Tree*. And I, who am supposed to influence my fellow citizens by setting them a good example, have all this dirt thrown at me. Well, I'm not standing for it. I'm not used to having my name dragged in the mud like this.

AUNE: Oh, you don't need to bother about that kind of thing, Mr Bernick.

BERNICK: Just now I do. I need all the respect and goodwill I can muster from my fellow citizens. I've big plans afoot, as I daresay you've heard, and if malicious-minded people succeed in shaking the community's trust in me, it could cause me very great difficulties. So I want at all costs to avoid giving these damned scribblers any food for gossip, and that's why I say the job's got to be done by the day after tomorrow.

AUNE: Mr Bernick, you might as well tell me it's got to be done by this afternoon.

BERNICK: You mean I'm demanding the impossible?

AUNE: With our present labour strength, yes.

BERNICK: Very well. Then I'll have to start looking elsewhere.

AUNE: You don't mean you're going to dismiss still more of the older men?

BERNICK: No, that's not what I was thinking.

AUNE: It'd create bad feeling in the town if you did that. And in the newspapers.

BERNICK: Probably it might, so I won't. But if the *Indian Girl* isn't ready to sail by the day after tomorrow, there'll be a notice of dismissal served on you.

AUNE: On me! (*Laughs*) You're joking, sir.

BERNICK: I shouldn't take that for granted if I were you.

AUNE: Dismiss me? But my father and his father worked all their lives in this yard. And so have I.

BERNICK: Who's making me do this?

AUNE: You're asking the impossible, Mr Bernick.

BERNICK: A good worker doesn't know the meaning of the

word impossible. Yes or no? Give me a straight answer, or you'll get your notice now.

AUNE (*takes a step towards him*): Mr Bernick, have you ever seriously thought what it means to give an old worker the sack? You think he can look round for something else? Oh, yes; he can do that; but that isn't the whole story. You ought to be present some time in a workman's house on the evening when he comes home and throws down his bag of tools behind the door.

BERNICK: Do you think I'm finding it easy to do this? Haven't I always been a good master to you?

AUNE: So much the worse for me, sir. It means no one at home will put the blame on you. They won't say anything to my face—they wouldn't dare—but they'll shoot a glance at me when they think I'm not looking and say to themselves: "Oh well, he must have deserved it." Don't you see, sir, that's the one thing I can't bear! Poor as I am, I've always been used to being regarded as lord and master in my own house. My humble home is a little community just as yours is, Mr Bernick, and I've been able to sustain it and keep it going because my wife has believed in me and my children have believed in me. And now it's all going to fall to the ground.

BERNICK: Well, if there's no alternative the lesser must make way for the greater. The individual must be sacrificed for the common cause. That's the only answer I can give you; it's the way of the world. You're a stubborn man, Aune. You oppose me, not because you must but because you won't accept the fact that machines can work better than flesh and blood.

AUNE: And you're so dead set on this, Mr Bernick, because you know that if you sack me at least you'll have shown the press you're anxious to do as they say you should.

BERNICK: Well, suppose I am? I've told you how much this means to me; either I have every newspaper in the district putting me in the pillory, or else I get them on my side just at the moment when I'm working to get a big project under way for the good of the community. Well then, how else can I act? My choice is either to keep your home going or to suppress the building of hundreds of new homes—hundreds of homes that will never be built, never have a fire in their hearth, unless I succeed in achieving what I'm now working for. Well, I leave the choice to you.

AUNE: I see. In that case I've no more to say.

BERNICK: Hm. My dear Aune, it really grieves me deeply that we have to part.

AUNE: We're not parting, Mr Bernick.

BERNICK: What do you mean?

AUNE: Working men have a sense of honour too.

BERNICK: Of course they have. Then you think you can promise—?

AUNE: The *Indian Girl* will be ready to sail the day after tomorrow.

Touches his forehead and goes out right.

BERNICK: Well, I've made that obstinate old fool see sense. That's a good omen, anyway.

HILMAR TOENNESEN *enters through the garden gate, smoking a cigar.*

HILMAR (*on the verandah*): Morning, Betty. Morning, Bernick.

MRS BERNICK: Good morning.

HILMAR: You've been crying. You know, then?

MRS BERNICK: Know what?

HILMAR: That the scandal's started. Ugh!

BERNICK: What do you mean?

HILMAR (*comes into the room*): Those two Americans are walking round the town in broad daylight with our little Dina Dorf.

MRS BERNICK (*follows him*): Hilmar, you're joking!

HILMAR: I'm afraid it's the truth. Lona was actually so tactless as to shout at me. Of course I pretended not to hear her.

BERNICK: And I suppose this hasn't exactly passed unnoticed.

HILMAR: You bet your life it hasn't. People stood still and stared at them. The news spread through the town like wildfire; like a prairie blaze. In every house people stood at their windows and waited for the procession to pass; they were packed behind their curtains like sardines—ugh! You must forgive me, Betty; I can't help saying "Ugh!," this makes me so nervous. If it goes on, I shall have to think about taking a holiday. Rather a long one.

MRS BERNICK: But you ought to have spoken to him and made it clear that—

HILMAR: What, in public? No, I'm sorry! But fancy him daring to show his face in this town at all! Well, we'll see if the newspapers can't put a spoke in his wheel. I'm sorry, Betty, but—

BERNICK: The newspapers, did you say? Have you heard anything to suggest that they may take action?

HILMAR: Oh yes, there's no doubt about that. When I left you yesterday afternoon, I took a walk up to the Club, for my health. It was quite evident from the silence that fell when I entered that they'd been talking about our American friends. Well, then that tactless editor fellow—you know, Hammer—came in and congratulated me out loud on my rich cousin's return home.

BERNICK: Rich—?

HILMAR: Yes, that's what he said. Of course I gave him a pretty piercing look and made it quite clear that I knew nothing about any riches as far as Johan Toennesen was concerned. "Oh, really?" he said. "That's strange. People usually do all right in America provided they have some capital, and your cousin didn't go empty-handed, did he?"

BERNICK: Hm. Look, do me the goodness to—

MRS BERNICK (*worried*): There you are, Karsten—

HILMAR: Yes, well anyway, he's given me a sleepless night. And he has the cheek to stroll round this town looking as innocent as an angel. Why didn't that illness he had knock him off? It's really monstrous how indestructible some people are.

MRS BERNICK: Hilmar, what are you saying?

HILMAR: Oh, I'm not saying anything. But look at him, he's survived railway accidents and attacks by grizzlies and

Blackfoot Indians without a scratch to show for it all. Didn't even get scalped. Ugh, here they are!

BERNICK (*glances up the street*): Olaf's with them!

HILMAR: But of course! They want to remind everyone that they belong to the best family in town. Look at all those people coming out of the chemist's to stare at them and make remarks. My nerves won't stand this. How a man can be expected to keep the flag of ideals flying under circumstances like these I really don't know—

BERNICK: They're coming here. Now listen, Betty, it's my express wish that you treat them with every courtesy.

MRS BERNICK: May I, Karsten?

BERNICK: Yes, yes; and you too, Hilmar. With luck they won't stay long, and while we're alone together I don't want there to be any insinuations. We must on no account embarrass them.

MRS BERNICK: Oh, Karsten, how magnanimous you are!

BERNICK: Yes, well; never mind that.

MRS BERNICK: No, you must let me thank you. And forgive me for becoming so emotional just now. Oh, you were quite justified in—

BERNICK: Never mind, I say, never *mind*.

HILMAR: Ugh!

JOHAN TOENNESEN *and* DINA *enter through the garden, followed by* MISS HESSEL *and* OLAF.

MISS HESSEL: Morning, everyone.

JOHAN: We've been giving the old place the once-over, Karsten.

BERNICK: Yes, so I hear. Plenty of changes, eh?

MISS HESSEL: Everywhere there's evidence of Karsten Bernick's great and good works. We've been around the gardens you presented to the town—

BERNICK: Oh, you've been there?

MISS HESSEL: "The Gift of Karsten Bernick," it says over the entrance. Yes, you seem to be the king-pin here all right.

JOHAN: Fine ships you've got too. I ran into the captain of the *Palm Tree*—he's an old school friend of mine—

52

MISS HESSEL: And you've built a new school; and I hear we can thank you for the waterworks and the gas tank.

BERNICK: Well, one must do something for the community one lives in.

MISS HESSEL: The sentiment does you credit, brother-in-law. It made me proud to see what a high opinion everyone has of you. I don't reckon myself vain, but I couldn't resist reminding one or two people we spoke to that Johan and I belong to the family.

HILMAR: Ugh!

MISS HESSEL: What's "Ugh!" about that?

HILMAR: All I said was "Hm!"

MISS HESSEL: Did you? Oh, that's all right. Well, you don't seem to have any visitors today.

MRS BERNICK: No, we're alone.

MISS HESSEL: We met a couple of your Salvationists in the market-place. They seemed to be in a great hurry. But we haven't had a real chance to talk yet, have we? Yesterday you had those three Railway Kings and the Reverend—

HILMAR: Schoolmaster.

MISS HESSEL: Well, I call him Reverend. But tell me, what do you think of what I've been doing for the past fifteen years? Hasn't he grown into a fine boy? Who'd ever think he was the same as that young good-for-nothing who ran away from home?

HILMAR: Hm.

JOHAN: Oh Lona, stop boasting.

MISS HESSEL: O.K., so I'm proud of it! Hell, it's the only thing I've ever achieved in the world; but it makes me feel I've done something to justify my existence. Yes, Johan, when I think how you and I started out there, with just our four bare paws—

HILMAR: Hands—

MISS HESSEL: I said paws. They were black.

HILMAR: Ugh!

MISS HESSEL: Yes, and empty.

HILMAR: Empty? Well, I must say—

MISS HESSEL: What must you say?

53

BERNICK *coughs.*

HILMAR: I must say—ugh! (*Goes out on to the verandah*)

MISS HESSEL: What's the matter with him?

BERNICK: Oh, never mind him; he's been rather nervous these last few days. Er—wouldn't you like to have a look round the garden? You haven't seen it properly yet, and I happen to have an hour free just now.

MISS HESSEL: That's a fine idea. I'd love to.

MRS BERNICK: There've been some big changes there too, as you'll see.

BERNICK, MRS BERNICK *and* MISS HESSEL *descend into the garden. We see them occasionally during the following scene.*

OLAF (*in the doorway to the verandah*): Uncle Hilmar, do you know what Uncle Johan asked me? He asked if I'd like to go with him to America.

HILMAR: You, you jackass? Why, you spend your whole time clinging to your mother's petticoats.

OLAF: I don't want to do that any longer. You wait—once I'm big, I'll—!

HILMAR: Oh, stuff! You've no stomach for danger.

They go together into the garden.

JOHAN (*to* DINA, *who has taken off her hat and is standing in the doorway on the right, shaking the dust from her dress*): I'm afraid that walk must have made you very hot.

DINA: No, I enjoyed it. I've never enjoyed a walk so much before.

JOHAN: You don't often go for walks in the morning, perhaps?

DINA: Oh, yes. But only with Olaf.

JOHAN: I see. Er—perhaps you'd rather go into the garden than stay inside here?

DINA: No, I'd rather stay here.

JOHAN: So would I. Good, that's agreed then, we'll take a walk like this every morning.

DINA: No, Mr Toennesen. You mustn't.

JOHAN: Mustn't? But you promised—

54

DINA: Yes, but now I think about it— you ought not to be seen with me.

JOHAN: But why not?

DINA: Oh, you're a stranger here. You don't understand. I'm not—

JOHAN: Yes?

DINA: No, I'd rather not talk about it.

JOHAN: Come on. You can tell me.

DINA: Well, if you want to know—I'm not like other girls. There's something—well, something. So you mustn't.

JOHAN: Look, I don't understand this at all. You haven't done anything wrong, have you?

DINA: No—*I* haven't—but—no, I don't want to talk any more about it. You'll hear all about it from the others, I expect.

JOHAN: Hm.

DINA: But there was something else I wanted to ask you.

JOHAN: What?

DINA: Is it as easy as they say to become—someone—over there in America?

JOHAN: No, it isn't always easy. You often have to work your fingers to the bone at first, and live pretty rough.

DINA: I wouldn't mind that.

JOHAN: You?

DINA: I can work. I'm healthy and strong, and Aunt Martha's taught me a lot.

JOHAN: Well, for heaven's sake then, come back with us.

DINA: Oh, you're only joking. You said that to Olaf. But tell me one thing. Are people as—as moral over there as they are here?

JOHAN: Moral?

DINA: Yes. I mean—are they as good and virtuous as they are here?

JOHAN: Well, they haven't all got horns, the way people here seem to imagine. You needn't be afraid of that.

DINA: You don't understand. I want to go somewhere where people aren't good and virtuous.

JOHAN: Where they *aren't*? What do you want them to be, then?

55

DINA: I want them to be natural.

JOHAN: They're that all right.

DINA: Then I think it'd be good for me if I could go and live there.

JOHAN: I'm sure it would. You must come back with us.

DINA: No, I don't want to go with you. I must go alone. Oh, I'd manage. I'd make something of myself—

BERNICK (*below the verandah with the two* LADIES): No, no, stay here, Betty dear. I'll fetch it. You might easily catch cold.

He enters the room and starts looking for MRS BERNICK'S *shawl.*

MRS BERNICK (*in the garden*): You must come with us, Johan. We're going down to the grotto.

BERNICK: No, I'm sure Johan would rather stay here. Dina, take my wife's shawl down to her, will you, and go along with them? Johan'll stay here with me, Betty dear. I want to hear about what life is like on the other side.

MRS BERNICK: All right, but come soon. You know where we'll be.

MRS BERNICK, MISS HESSEL *and* DINA *go out left through the garden.*

BERNICK (*watches them go for a moment, then walks across to the door upstage left and closes it. Then he goes over to* JOHAN, *clasps both his hands, shakes and presses them*): Johan! Now we're alone—thank you! Thank you!

JOHAN: Oh, nonsense.

BERNICK: My house and home, the happiness of my family, my position in the community—I owe it all to you.

JOHAN: Well, I'm glad to hear it, my dear Karsten. Some good came out of that silly business after all, then.

BERNICK (*shakes his hands again*): Thank you, thank you! There isn't one man in ten thousand who'd have done as you did.

JOHAN: Forget it! We were both young and wild, weren't we? One of us had to take the rap.

BERNICK: But who deserved to, if not the guilty one?

JOHAN: Now wait a minute! On this occasion it was the inno-

56

cent one who deserved the rap. I had no worries or responsibilities; and no parents. I was glad of a chance to get away from that drudgery at the office. You had your old mother still alive; besides, you'd just got secretly engaged to Betty, and she was deeply in love with you. What would have happened to her if she'd found out that you—?

BERNICK: I know, I know; all the same—

JOHAN: And wasn't it just for Betty's sake that you broke off that business with Mrs Dorf? You'd only gone along that evening to put an end to it all—

BERNICK: Yes; why did that drunken ruffian have to come home just that evening? Yes, Johan, it was for Betty's sake; even so—that you could be so unselfish as to take the blame on yourself, and go away—

JOHAN: Forget it, my dear Karsten. After all, we agreed that this was the best solution; we had to get you out of it somehow, and you were my friend. Yes, how proud I was of that friendship! I was a poor country lad working in an office, you were rich and of good family, just back from Paris and London—and yet you chose me as your friend, though I was four years younger than you. Oh, I realize now it was because you were in love with Betty, but how proud I was! And who wouldn't have been? Who wouldn't gladly have sacrificed himself for you, especially when all it meant was giving the town something to gossip about for a month and having an excuse to get away from it all into the great wide world outside?

BERNICK: Hm. My dear Johan, to be frank I must tell you that the matter hasn't quite been forgotten yet.

JOHAN: Hasn't it? Well, what's that to me? Once I'm back on my ranch—

BERNICK: You're going back, then?

JOHAN: Of course.

BERNICK: But not too soon, I hope?

JOHAN: As soon as I can. I only came here to please Lona.

BERNICK: Oh? How do you mean?

JOHAN: Well, you see, Lona isn't young any longer, and these last few months she's been pining her heart out to get back

57

here; but she wouldn't ever admit it. (*Smiles*) She didn't dare leave an irresponsible young fellow like me on my own, when by the age of nineteen I'd already gone and—

BERNICK: Yes, well?

JOHAN: Karsten, I've got a confession to make to you which I'm a little ashamed about.

BERNICK: You didn't tell her?

JOHAN: Yes, I did. It was wrong of me, but I had to. You've no idea what Lona has been to me. I know you could never get along with her, but to me she's been like a mother. Those first years over there, when we were so poor—you've no idea how she worked! And when I had that long illness and couldn't earn anything, she went off and sang in cafés—I tried to stop her but I couldn't—and gave lectures which people laughed at, and wrote a book which she's since laughed over herself—yes, and cried over—all just to keep me alive. I couldn't sit there last winter and watch her pining her heart out after the way she'd slaved and toiled for me. Karsten, I couldn't! So I said to her: "Go, Lona. You needn't worry about me. I'm not as irresponsible as you think." And then—well, I told her.

BERNICK: And how did she take it?

JOHAN: Well, she quite rightly decided that since I'd proved myself innocent there was no reason why I shouldn't come back with her. But you don't need to worry. Lona won't talk, and I can keep my mouth shut. Like I did before.

BERNICK: Oh, yes, yes. I trust you.

JOHAN: Here's my hand on it. Well now, we'll say no more about that business; luckily it's the only crazy thing either of us has ever done. I intend to enjoy the few days I'm going to be here. You can't imagine what a lovely walk we had this morning. Who'd ever have imagined that that little girl who used to run around here and act cherubs at the theatre would ever—by the way, Karsten, what happened to her parents—afterwards?

BERNICK: My dear chap, I don't know any more than what I wrote to you just after you sailed. You got my two letters all right?

58

JOHAN: Yes, yes, I have both of them. That drunken scoundrel left her, then?

BERNICK: Yes, and got himself killed in a brawl.

JOHAN: She died not long afterwards, didn't she? But you did all you could for her, I presume? Secretly, I mean?

BERNICK: She was proud. She revealed nothing, and refused to accept a penny.

JOHAN: You did the right thing in bringing Dina to live with you.

BERNICK: Of course, of course. Actually, it was Martha who arranged that.

JOHAN: Was it Martha? Yes, by the way, where is Martha today?

BERNICK: Where is she? Oh, when she isn't at the school she's busy with her invalids.

JOHAN: So it was Martha who took care of her?

BERNICK: Yes, Martha's always had rather a weakness for looking after children. That was why she took this job at the council school. Damn stupid idea.

JOHAN: Yes, she looked pretty worn-out yesterday. I'm afraid you're right, she isn't really strong enough for that kind of work.

BERNICK: Oh, she's strong enough for it. But it's so unpleasant for me. It makes it look as though I wasn't prepared to maintain my own sister.

JOHAN: Maintain her? I thought she had money of her own—

BERNICK: Not a penny. You remember what a difficult situation mother was in when you left? Well, she managed to keep going for a while, with my help, but I wasn't really happy with that as a long-term policy. I thought I'd go in with her, but even that wasn't enough. In the end, I had to take over the whole business, and when we finally drew up the accounts there was scarcely anything left of mother's share. Soon afterwards she died and of course Martha was left practically penniless.

JOHAN: Poor Martha!

BERNICK: Poor? What do you mean? You don't imagine I let her want for anything? Oh no, I think I may say I'm a good brother to her. She lives with us, naturally, and eats at our table; her teacher's salary is sufficient for her clothing needs, and—well, she's a single woman, what more does she want?

JOHAN: Hm; we don't reason like that in America.

BERNICK: No, I dare say not, in an unstable society like theirs. But here in our little community, which immorality hasn't yet, thank God, begun to corrupt, the women are content to occupy a modest and unassuming position. Anyway, it's Martha's own fault; she could have been provided for long ago, if she'd been so minded.

JOHAN: Could have married, you mean?

BERNICK: Yes, and very advantageously. She's had several good offers; strangely enough, considering she's a woman with no money and no longer young, and really rather ordinary.

JOHAN: Ordinary?

BERNICK: Oh, don't think I hold it against her. Indeed, I wouldn't have it otherwise. You know how it is, in a big house like ours it's always useful to have a—well—placid-natured person around whom one can ask to do anything.

JOHAN: Yes, but what about her?

BERNICK: What do you mean, what about her? Oh, I see. Well, she's got plenty to interest herself; she's got me and Betty and Olaf and—me. It isn't good for people to be always thinking of themselves first, least of all women. After all, each of us has a community of one kind or another to work for, be it great or small. I do so, anyway. (*Indicates* KRAP, *as the latter enters right*) Here's an example for you. This business I have to deal with now, do you suppose it's to do with my own company? Not a bit of it. (*Quickly, to* KRAP) Well?

KRAP (*shows him a sheaf of papers and whispers*): All the documents for the transaction are in order.

BERNICK: Good! Splendid! Well, brother-in-law, I'm afraid you'll have to excuse me for a while. (*Lowers his voice as he presses his hand*) Thank you, Johan, thank you! You may rest assured that anything I can ever do for you—well, you understand. (*To* KRAP) Come with me.

They go into BERNICK'S *office.*

JOHAN (*looks after him for a moment*): Hm.

He turns to go down into the garden. As he does so, MARTHA
enters right with a small basket on her arm.

JOHAN: Why, Martha!
MARTHA: Oh—Johan—is it you?
JOHAN: You've been out early too.
MARTHA: Yes. Wait here a minute, I'm sure the others will be
along soon.

Turns to go out, left.

JOHAN: Look, Martha, are you always in such a hurry?
MARTHA: Am I—?
JOHAN: Yesterday you seemed to be avoiding me—I didn't
manage to get a word with you—and today—
MARTHA: Yes, but—
JOHAN: We always used to be inseparable. Ever since we
were children.
MARTHA: Oh, Johan. That's many, many years ago.
JOHAN: For heaven's sake! It's only fifteen years. You think
I've changed?
MARTHA: You? Oh yes—you have too—although—
JOHAN: What do you mean?
MARTHA: Oh, nothing.
JOHAN: You don't sound very glad to see me again.
MARTHA: I've waited so long, Johan. Too long.
JOHAN: Waited? For me to come back?
MARTHA: Yes.
JOHAN: Why did you think I'd want to come back?
MARTHA: To repair the wrong you did.
JOHAN: I?
MARTHA: Have you forgotten that a woman died in destitu-
tion and disgrace because of you? Have you forgotten that
because of you the best years of a young child's life were
embittered?
JOHAN: You don't mean that you—? Martha, did your brother
never—?

61

MARTHA: Do what?

JOHAN: Did he never—I mean—did he never say anything in mitigation of what I did?

MARTHA: Oh, Johan, you know how strict Karsten's principles are.

JOHAN: Hm. Yes, yes, I know how strict my old friend Karsten's principles are. But this is—! Oh, well. I spoke to him just now. I think he's changed somewhat.

MARTHA: How can you say that? Karsten has always been a fine man.

JOHAN: Yes, I didn't mean it like that; but never mind. Hm! Well, now I understand how you've been thinking about me. You've been awaiting the return of the prodigal.

MARTHA: Listen, Johan. I'll tell you how I've been thinking about you. (*Points down into the garden*) You see that girl playing down there on the grass with Olaf? That is Dina. You remember that strange letter you wrote to me when you ran away? You wrote that I must believe in you. I have believed in you, Johan. Those wicked things people talked about afterwards—you did them in a fit of madness, you didn't know what you were doing—

JOHAN: What do you mean?

MARTHA: Oh, you know what I mean; don't let's talk about it any more. Anyway, you had to go away and start—a new life. Listen, Johan. You remember how we two used to play games together when we were children? Well, I have acted as your proxy here. The duties that you forgot to fulfil here, or couldn't fulfil, I have fulfilled for you. I tell you this so that you shan't have that to reproach yourself with too. I have been a mother to that wronged child; I've brought her up, as well as I could—

JOHAN: And wasted your whole life for her sake.

MARTHA: It hasn't been wasted. But you took so long in coming, Johan.

JOHAN: Martha—if only I could tell you the—! Well, anyway let me thank you for being such a loyal friend to me.

MARTHA (*smiles sadly*): Hm. Well, now we've had our talk, Johan. Hush, someone's coming. Goodbye. I can't wait now.

She goes out through the door upstage left. MISS HESSEL *enters from the garden, followed by* MRS BERNICK.

MRS BERNICK (*still in the garden*): For heaven's sake, Lona, what are you thinking of?

MISS HESSEL: Let me go! I tell you I must speak with him.

MRS BERNICK: But it'd create the most dreadful scandal. Oh, Johan, are you still here?

MISS HESSEL: Get along now, son. Don't stand hanging round indoors; go down into the garden and talk to Dina.

JOHAN: Yes, I was just thinking of doing that.

MRS BERNICK: But—

MISS HESSEL: Johan, have you bothered to take a close look at Dina?

JOHAN: Why, yes, I think so.

MISS HESSEL: So you damn well should. Now there *is* something for you.

MRS BERNICK: But Lona—!

JOHAN: Something for me?

MISS HESSEL: Yes, well, something to look at, anyway. O.K., then, get going!

JOHAN: Yes, yes, I'm going. I'm going!

He goes down into the garden.

MRS BERNICK: Lona, I'm speechless! Surely you can't be serious about this?

MISS HESSEL: Of course I'm serious! She's a healthy, honest girl, and in her right mind, isn't she? She'd make just the wife for Johan. That's the kind of girl he needs over there, not an old half-sister.

MRS BERNICK: Dina! Dina Dorf! But Lona, think—

MISS HESSEL: All I'm thinking about is the boy's happiness. He needs me to give him a push, he's a bit timid where these things are concerned; never really had an eye for girls.

MRS BERNICK: What, Johan? I should have thought we had sufficient evidence to the contrary—unfortunately—

MISS HESSEL: Oh, to hell with that, that's ancient history! Where's Karsten? I want to talk to him.

MRS BERNICK: Lona, you mustn't do this, I tell you.

MISS HESSEL: I'm going to do it. If the boy likes her, and she likes him, let them have one another. Karsten's a clever guy, he'll manage to find a way—

MRS BERNICK: Do you really imagine that these American improprieties will be permitted here?

MISS HESSEL: Betty, don't talk nonsense.

MRS BERNICK: And that a man with such strict moral principles as Karsten—

MISS HESSEL: Oh, nonsense, they're not that strict.

MRS BERNICK: How dare you!

MISS HESSEL: All I'm saying is that Karsten isn't any more moral than most other men.

MRS BERNICK: You still hate him, don't you? But what do you want here, if you can't forget—? I don't understand how you dare to look him in the face after the disgraceful way you behaved towards him.

MISS HESSEL: Yes, Betty, I did overstep the mark a bit that time.

MRS BERNICK: And he's forgiven you so generously, though he never did you any wrong. It wasn't his fault that you set your cap at him. But ever since that moment you've hated me too. (*Bursts into tears*) You've always begrudged me my happiness. And now you come here to shame me, by showing the town what kind of a family I've made Karsten marry into! I'm the person everyone will blame, and that's what you want. Oh, it's hateful of you! (*She goes out weeping through the door upstage left*)

MISS HESSEL (*watches her go*): Poor Betty!

BERNICK *enters from his office.*

BERNICK (*still in the doorway*): Yes, yes, Krap. Good. Excellent. Send four hundred crowns to provide food for the poor. (*Turns*) Lona! (*Comes closer*) Are you alone? Isn't Betty with you?

MISS HESSEL: No. Shall I go and fetch her?

BERNICK: No, no, it doesn't matter. Oh, Lona, you can't

imagine how I've been longing for a chance to talk frankly with you. To ask your forgiveness.

MISS HESSEL: Look, Karsten, don't let's get sentimental. It doesn't suit us.

BERNICK: You must listen to me, Lona. I know appearances seem to be against me now that you know about Dina's mother. But I swear to you it was only a temporary infatuation. I did love you once, honestly and truly.

MISS HESSEL: Why do you think I've come back?

BERNICK: Whatever you have in mind, I beseech you not to do anything before you have given me the chance to vindicate myself. I can, Lona; at any rate I can explain to you why I acted as I did.

MISS HESSEL: Now you're afraid. You once loved me, you say. Yes, you told me so often enough in your letters—and perhaps it was true in a way, as long as you were living out there in a world which was big and free and gave you the courage to think bigly and freely yourself. You probably thought I had a bit more character and will and independence than most of the others here. Besides, it was a secret between the two of us; no one could make funny remarks about your vulgar taste.

BERNICK: Lona, how can you think that—?

MISS HESSEL: But when you came back here and heard how people were laughing at me, and making fun of what they called my peculiarities—

BERNICK: Well, you were rather headstrong in those days.

MISS HESSEL: Only because I wanted to shock the prudes this town was full of—the ones in trousers as well as the ones in petticoats. Well, then you met that charming young actress—

BERNICK: It was a momentary infatuation, nothing more. I swear to you that not a tenth part of all the rumours and slander that went round about me was true.

MISS HESSEL: Possibly. But then Betty came home, pretty and rich, and everyone's darling; and the news got around that she was to inherit all her aunt's money and I was to get nothing—

BERNICK: Yes, that was the crux of it, Lona. I shan't beat

about the bush. I didn't love Betty; I didn't break with you because my affections had changed. It was only for the money. I needed it; I *had* to make sure I got it.

MISS HESSEL: And you can tell me that to my face!

BERNICK: Yes, I do. Please listen to me, Lona—

MISS HESSEL: But you wrote to me that you'd fallen passionately in love with Betty, asked me to be magnanimous, begged me for Betty's sake to say nothing about the fact that there had been anything between us—

BERNICK: I had to, I tell you.

MISS HESSEL: Then, by God, I don't regret what I did.

BERNICK: Let me explain to you calmly and objectively how things stood. My mother, you recall, was head of the family business; but she had no business sense whatever. I was urgently summoned home from Paris; things had become critical; I had to get the firm back on its feet again. What did I find? I found a business tottering on the verge of bankruptcy. We had to keep it absolutely secret, of course, but this ancient and respected house which had flourished for three generations was facing ruin. I was her son, her only son. I had to look round for some means of saving it.

MISS HESSEL: So you saved the House of Bernick at the expense of a woman.

BERNICK: You know quite well that Betty loved me.

MISS HESSEL: What about me?

BERNICK: Believe me, Lona, you would never have been happy with me.

MISS HESSEL: Was it out of consideration for my happiness that you jilted me?

BERNICK: You think I acted from selfish motives? If it had only been my interests that had been at stake, I would gladly and fearlessly have started again from nothing. But you don't understand how a man of business identifies himself with the business he inherits and with the vast responsibilities it brings with it. Do you realize that the happiness or misery of hundreds, even thousands of people depends on him? Has it ever occurred to you that the whole of our

66

community, which both you and I call our home, would have been shattered if the House of Bernick had failed?

MISS HESSEL: Is it also for the sake of the community that for the past fifteen years your life has been based upon a lie?

BERNICK: A lie?

MISS HESSEL: How much does Betty know about the circumstances that lay behind her marriage with you?

BERNICK: Do you really believe I'd hurt her by revealing such things? What dividends would that pay?

MISS HESSEL: What dividends, did you say? Ah, well, you're a business man—I suppose you know best about dividends. Now listen to me, Karsten. I'm going to talk calmly and objectively to you. Tell me; are you really happy?

BERNICK: In my family life, you mean?

MISS HESSEL: Of course.

BERNICK: Yes, Lona, I am. The sacrifice you made for me wasn't in vain. I think I can say I've grown happier year by year. Betty's so good and acquiescent. During the years we've lived together she has learned to mould her character to mine—

MISS HESSEL: Hm.

BERNICK: She used to have a lot of over-romantic ideas about love; she couldn't accept that as the years pass it must shrink into the calm candle-flame of friendship.

MISS HESSEL: But she accepts that now?

BERNICK: Completely. As you can imagine, her daily association with me hasn't been without a maturing influence on her. People have to learn to reduce their demands on each other if they are to fulfil their functions in the community in which it has pleased God to place them. Betty has gradually learned to realize this, with the result that our house is now an example to our fellow citizens.

MISS HESSEL: But these fellow citizens know nothing about this lie?

BERNICK: Lie?

MISS HESSEL: Yes, the lie on which your life has been resting for the past fifteen years.

BERNICK: You call that a—?

67

MISS HESSEL: I call it a lie. A triple lie. You lied to me, you lied to Betty and you lied to Johan.

BERNICK: Betty has never asked to be told the truth.

MISS HESSEL: Because she doesn't know.

BERNICK: And you won't ask it. For her sake you won't.

MISS HESSEL: Oh, no. I can put up with ridicule; I've a broad back.

BERNICK: Johan won't, either. He's told me so.

MISS HESSEL: But what about you, Karsten? Isn't there something in you that cries out to be freed from this lie?

BERNICK: Do you expect me voluntarily to sacrifice the happiness of my family and my position in society?

MISS HESSEL: What right have you to that position?

BERNICK: Every day for the past fifteen years I have purchased a grain of that right—by my conduct, and my work, and my achievements.

MISS HESSEL: Yes, you've achieved plenty all right—for yourself and for others. You're the richest and most powerful man in town; no one dares oppose you, because you're supposed to be a man without fault or dishonour; your home is regarded as a pattern for other homes; your career as an example for other men to follow. But all this honour, and you too, rest on a quicksand. A moment may come, a word may be spoken, and you and all your honour will sink to the bottom, if you don't save yourself in time.

BERNICK: Why have you come, Lona?

MISS HESSEL: I want to help you to get firm ground under your feet, Karsten.

BERNICK: Revenge! You want revenge? Yes, that's it, of course. But you won't succeed! There's only one person who knows the truth, and he'll hold his tongue.

MISS HESSEL: Johan?

BERNICK: Yes, Johan. If anyone else accuses me, I shall deny everything. If anyone tries to destroy me, I shall fight for my life! You'll never succeed, I tell you! The only person who could destroy me is silent. And he's going away.

RUMMEL *and* VIGELAND *enter right*.

RUMMEL: Good morning, good morning, my dear Bernick. You must come along with us to the Chamber of Commerce. You know, to discuss the railway.

BERNICK: I can't. Not just now.

VIGELAND: But Mr Bernick, you must—!

RUMMEL: You must, Bernick. There are people working against us. That damned newspaper editor, Hammer, and the others who wanted the coast line, are saying there are private interests behind this new proposal.

BERNICK: Well, tell them—

VIGELAND: It won't help what *we* tell them, Mr Bernick.

RUMMEL: No, no, you must come yourself. No one will dare to suspect you of anything like that.

MISS HESSEL: Why, the very idea!

BERNICK: I can't, I tell you. I'm not well. That is—well, anyway, wait a minute and give me time to collect myself.

ROERLUND *enters right.*

ROERLUND: Excuse me, Mr Bernick. I've just seen something that has deeply disturbed me.

BERNICK: Yes, yes, what is it?

ROERLUND: I must ask you a question. Is it with your consent that the young girl who has found asylum beneath your roof is walking the public streets in the company of a person who—

MISS HESSEL: What person, Reverend?

ROERLUND: Of the person from whom, of all people, she should be kept at the greatest possible distance.

MISS HESSEL *laughs loudly.*

ROERLUND: Is it with your consent, Mr Bernick?

BERNICK (*looks for his hat and gloves*): I know nothing about it. Excuse me, I'm in a hurry—I have to attend a meeting of the Chamber of Commerce.

HILMAR (*enters from the garden and goes over to the door upstage left*): Betty, Betty!

MRS BERNICK (*in the doorway*): What is it?

HILMAR: You really must go down into the garden and put a

stop to the way a certain person is flirting with Dina Dorf. It made me quite nervous to listen to them.

MISS HESSEL: Oh? What did this person say?

HILMAR: Only that he wants her to go with him to America! Ugh!

ROERLUND: Can this be possible!

MRS BERNICK: What are you saying!

MISS HESSEL: But it'd be a wonderful thing!

BERNICK: Impossible. You must have misheard.

HILMAR: Ask him yourself, then. Here come the happy pair. Keep me out of it, though.

BERNICK (*to* RUMMEL *and* VIGELAND): Go ahead, I'll join you in a moment.

RUMMEL *and* VIGELAND *go out right.* JOHAN *and* DINA *enter from the garden.*

JOHAN: Lona, Lona, she's coming with us!

MRS BERNICK: Johan, you must be mad!

ROERLUND: I refuse to believe my ears! This is the most disgraceful scandal! By what arts of seduction have you—?

JOHAN: Now, take it easy—!

ROERLUND: Answer me, Dina. Do you seriously intend to do this? Have you made this decision freely and voluntarily?

DINA: I must get away from here.

ROERLUND: But with him! With him!

DINA: Name me any other man here who would have the courage to take me away with him.

ROERLUND: Right, then you'll have to be told who he is.

JOHAN: Be quiet!

BERNICK: Don't say another word!

ROERLUND: If I remained silent I should be betraying the community whose moral and manners I have been chosen to protect; and I should be failing my duty towards this young girl in whose upbringing I have had no small share, and who is to me—

JOHAN: Be careful what you say!

ROERLUND: She shall know the truth! Dina, it was this man who was responsible for your mother's misery and shame.

BERNICK: Dr Roerlund!

DINA: He! (*To* JOHAN) Is this true?

JOHAN: Karsten, you answer her.

BERNICK: Silence, all of you! The subject is closed.

DINA: It is true, then.

ROERLUND: Of course it is true. And that's not all. This person in whom you have placed your trust did not leave home empty-handed. Old Mrs Bernick's money—her son can testify.

MISS HESSEL: Liar!

BERNICK: Ah!

MRS BERNICK: Oh, my God, my God!

JOHAN (*raises his arm*): You dare to—

MISS HESSEL: Don't hit him, Johan.

ROERLUND: Yes, go on, hit me! The truth shall out—and it is the truth—Mr Bernick has said so himself, and the whole town knows it. Well, Dina, now you know the kind of man he is.

Short silence.

JOHAN (*quietly, grips* BERNICK'S *arm*): Karsten, Karsten, what have you done?

MRS BERNICK (*in tears, softly*): Oh, Karsten, that I should have involved you in such a scandal!

SANDSTAD (*hurries in right and shouts, with his hand still on the door-handle*): Mr Bernick, you must come at once! The railway is hanging by a thread!

BERNICK (*abstractedly*): What? What must I do?

MISS HESSEL (*earnestly, meaningly*): You must do your duty to the community, brother-in-law.

SANDSTAD: Yes, hurry! We need all your moral authority behind us.

JOHAN (*close to* BERNICK): Bernick, you and I will talk about this tomorrow.

He goes out through the garden. BERNICK *helplessly and blindly walks out right with* SANDSTAD.

ACT THREE

The same. BERNICK *enters angrily through the door upstage left with a cane in his hand, leaving the door ajar behind him.*

BERNICK: There, now! He's been asking for that. I fancy he won't forget that hiding in a hurry. (*Speaks to someone through the open door*) What? Oh, Betty, you mother the boy too much. You make excuses for him and take his side whatever he does. Irresponsible little brat! Not irresponsible? What would you call it, then? Sneaking out of the house at night, stealing one of the fishermen's boats, stays away half the day and frightens the life out of me—! As if I hadn't enough on my mind already! And then the young puppy has the nerve to threaten me that he'll run away! Well, just let him try! You? No, I'm sure you don't; you don't care what happens to him. I really believe if he went and killed himself, you'd— Oh, don't you? Possibly, but when I die I shall leave something behind me that I want carried on; I don't fancy the idea of being left childless. Don't argue, Betty, I've given my orders; he's not to leave the house. (*Listens*) Be quiet now, I don't want anyone to notice anything.

KRAP enters right.

KRAP: Can you spare me a moment, Mr Bernick?
BERNICK (*throws down the cane*): Yes, yes, by all means. Have you come from the yard?
KRAP: Yes, I've just left there. Hm.
BERNICK: Well? Everything's going ahead all right with the *Palm Tree*, isn't it?
KRAP: Oh, the *Palm Tree* will be able to sail tomorrow, but—

BERNICK: Is it the *Indian Girl*? Don't tell me that stubborn old fool—

KRAP: The *Indian Girl* will be able to sail tomorrow too—but she won't get very far.

BERNICK: What do you mean?

KRAP: Excuse me, Mr Bernick, but that door's open and I think there's someone in there.

BERNICK (*closes the door*): Well, what have you got to tell me that mustn't be overheard?

KRAP: It's this. Your foreman seems determined to send the *Indian Girl* to the bottom with all hands.

BERNICK: Aune? Good God, what on earth makes you think that?

KRAP: Can't think of any other explanation, Mr Bernick.

BERNICK: Well, tell me. But be brief.

KRAP: Yes, Mr Bernick. Well, you know how slowly the work's been going since we got those new machines and took on those untrained workmen.

BERNICK: Yes, yes.

KRAP: But when I went down there this morning I noticed they'd made the most extraordinary progress on the American ship. That big patch on her hull—you know, where she's gone rotten—

BERNICK: Yes, yes, what about it?

KRAP: Completely repaired! Apparently. They've sheathed it. Looks as good as new. Aune himself had been working on her all night with a lantern.

BERNICK: Well?

KRAP: I thought about it. Didn't like it. The men were having lunch, so I went and took a good look at her, outside and in. No one saw me. I had difficulty in getting down into the hold, because they've reloaded the cargo, but I saw enough to confirm my suspicions. There's something funny going on, Mr Bernick.

BERNICK: You must be mistaken, Mr Krap. I can't believe Aune would do a thing like that.

KRAP: I don't like saying it, but it's the truth. Something funny going on, I said to myself. He hadn't put in any new

73

timbers, as far as I could see; just plugged and caulked her, and covered it up with plates and tarpaulins and so on. Real shoddy workmanship! The *Indian Girl* will never reach New York. She'll go to the bottom like a cracked kettle.

BERNICK: This is dreadful! But what motive do you suppose he can have?

KRAP: Probably wants to bring the machines into discredit. Revenge; wants to force you to take the old workmen back.

BERNICK: And for that he's willing to sacrifice all those human lives.

KRAP: He said the other day: "There aren't any human beings in the *Indian Girl*. Only beasts."

BERNICK: Possibly; but what about all the capital investment that will be lost? Hasn't he thought of that?

KRAP: Aune doesn't hold with capital investment, Mr Bernick.

BERNICK: True enough. He's a trouble-maker, a demagogue. All the same—to be so devoid of conscience—! Look here, Krap, we must check on this. Not a word about it to anyone. It'll be bad for the yard if this leaks out.

KRAP: Of course, but—

BERNICK: You must try to get down there again during the dinner break. I must have the truth about this.

KRAP: I'll get it for you, Mr Bernick. But may I ask—what will you do if—?

BERNICK: Report the matter, of course. We can't let ourselves be accessories to a criminal action. I can't afford to have that on my conscience. Besides, it will make a good impression on both the press and the community if they see that I am putting personal considerations aside so that justice may take its course.

KRAP: Very true, Mr Bernick.

BERNICK: But first we must have the truth. Meanwhile, not a word to anyone.

KRAP: You can trust me, Mr Bernick. I'll get the truth for you.

He goes out through the garden and down the street.

BERNICK (*to himself*): Terrible! But—no, it's impossible! It couldn't happen.

He turns to enter his office. HILMAR TOENNESEN *enters right.*

HILMAR: Morning, Bernick. Well, congratulations on your triumph at the Chamber of Commerce yesterday.

BERNICK: Oh, thank you.

HILMAR: Brilliant victory, they tell me. Public-spirited visionary routs chauvinistic self-interest. Like a colonial power disciplining the savages. Remarkable achievement after that unpleasant little scene you'd—

BERNICK: Yes, yes, never mind that.

HILMAR: I gather the final *coup de grâce* hasn't been delivered yet, though.

BERNICK: You mean the railway?

HILMAR: Yes. You know what our beloved editor Mr Hammer is cooking up, I presume?

BERNICK (*tensely*): No. What?

HILMAR: He's cottoned on to that rumour that's floating around. Says he's going to make it front-page news.

BERNICK: What rumour?

HILMAR: Why, all that buying up of property along the route of the branch line.

BERNICK: What? Is there a rumour to that effect?

HILMAR: Yes, it's all over town. I heard about it at the Club. It seems one of our lawyers has been secretly buying up all the forests and mines and waterfalls on behalf of an anonymous client.

BERNICK: Do they say who this client is?

HILMAR: The members thought he must be acting for a syndicate in some other town that had heard about your plans and thought they'd get in quickly before property values began to soar. Disgusting, isn't it, what? Ugh!

BERNICK: Disgusting?

HILMAR: Yes, absolute strangers trespassing on our property like that. And fancy one of our own lawyers lending himself to such a scheme! Now it'll be these damned outsiders who'll reap all the profit.

75

BERNICK: But it's only an unconfirmed rumour.

HILMAR: Yes, but everyone believes it, and tomorrow or the day after Hammer will publish it as a fact. Everyone at the Club's feeling very bitter about it already. I heard several people say that if the rumour's confirmed they'll withdraw their support.

BERNICK: But that's impossible!

HILMAR: Oh? Why do you suppose those hucksters were so keen to go in with you? Do you think they hadn't already started licking their lips at the—?

BERNICK: Impossible, I tell you! We have *some* public spirit in this little community—!

HILMAR: Here? Look, you're an optimist and you judge other people by yourself. But I know our town pretty well, and I tell you there isn't one person here—apart from ourselves, of course—not one, I tell you, who attempts to keep the flag of ideals flying. (*Upstage*) Ugh, here they are!

BERNICK: Who?

HILMAR: The two Americans. (*Looks out, right*) Who's that with them? Oh dear, isn't that the captain of the *Indian Girl*? Ugh!

BERNICK: What on earth can they want with him?

HILMAR: Birds of a feather, I suppose. He's probably been a pirate, or a slave-trader; and heaven knows what they haven't got up to in the past fifteen years.

BERNICK: No, you've no right to think of them like that.

HILMAR: You *are* an optimist. Well, if they're descending on us again, I'll be off.

He goes towards the door, left. MISS HESSEL *enters right.*

MISS HESSEL: Hullo, Hilmar. Am I chasing you away?

HILMAR: Not at all. I just happen to be in a hurry. I've something I have to say to Betty.

Enters the room upstage left.

BERNICK (*after a short silence*): Well, Lona?

MISS HESSEL: Well?

BERNICK: How do you feel about me today?

MISS HESSEL: The same as yesterday. One lie more or less—
BERNICK: I must make you understand. Where is Johan?
MISS HESSEL: He's coming. He had something he wanted to ask someone.
BERNICK: After what you heard yesterday, surely you must understand that everything I have built up here will be destroyed if the truth gets out.
MISS HESSEL: I understand that.
BERNICK: I need hardly tell you that I was not guilty of this theft which was rumoured to have been committed.
MISS HESSEL: Oh, naturally. But who was the thief, then?
BERNICK: There was no thief. No money was stolen. Not a penny was missing.
MISS HESSEL: What?
BERNICK: I repeat; not a penny.
MISS HESSEL: Then how did that monstrous rumour get round that Johan—?
BERNICK: Lona, I can talk to you as I wouldn't to anyone else. I shan't hide anything from you. I was partly responsible for spreading that rumour.
MISS HESSEL: You? You could do a thing like that to him, when to save your skin he'd—?
BERNICK: You mustn't judge me without remembering how things stood at the time. I explained it to you yesterday. I came home and found my mother involved in a whole string of stupid enterprises. One misfortune followed after another; every disaster that could happen to us happened; our house stood on the verge of ruin. I felt desperate and reckless. Oh, Lona, I think it was mainly in the hope of trying to forget it all that I got myself involved in that— business which ended in Johan going away.
MISS HESSEL: Hm.
BERNICK: You can imagine how all sorts of rumours spread about after you and he had left. It wasn't the first thing of that kind he'd done, they said; Dorf had been well paid to go away and keep his mouth shut; others said she'd been given the money. Just then it was beginning to get whispered that our house was having difficulty in fulfilling its

77

obligations. What more natural than that the scandal-mongers should put two and two together? When she stayed on here in obvious poverty, people said he'd taken the money with him to America; the gossip increased and the sum multiplied like a snowball.

MISS HESSEL: And you, Karsten—?

BERNICK: I seized on this rumour as a drowning man clutches at a raft.

MISS HESSEL: You encouraged it?

BERNICK: I didn't contradict it. Our creditors were beginning to get restive; I had to find some way of calming them; it was essential that no one should doubt our solidarity. We'd had a temporary setback; they mustn't foreclose on us; we only needed a little time, and everyone would get their money.

MISS HESSEL: And everyone got their money?

BERNICK: Yes, Lona. This rumour saved our house, and made me the man I am now.

MISS HESSEL: In other words, a lie made you the man you are now.

BERNICK: Who suffered by it—then? Johan had sworn he'd never come back.

MISS HESSEL: You ask who suffered by it. Look at yourself, Karsten, and tell me honestly; don't you think you've suffered?

BERNICK: Look at any man you choose to name; you'll find every one of them has at least one skeleton hidden in his cupboard.

MISS HESSEL: And you call yourselves pillars of society?

BERNICK: Society has none better.

MISS HESSEL: If that's what your society is like, what does it matter whether it survives or is destroyed? What do people here set store by? Lies and pretences—that's all. You, the chief citizen of the town, sit here in honour and happiness, power and glory, simply because you once branded an innocent man as a criminal.

BERNICK: Do you think I don't know how deeply I wronged him? And do you think I'm not ready to right that wrong?

MISS HESSEL: How? By talking?

BERNICK: I can't do that, Lona.

MISS HESSEL: How else can such a wrong be righted?

BERNICK: I am rich, Lona. Johan can ask anything he wants—

MISS HESSEL: Yes, offer him money, and see what he replies.

BERNICK: Do you know what he intends to do?

MISS HESSEL: No. Since yesterday he's said nothing. It's as though all this has suddenly made him into a man.

BERNICK: I must talk to him.

MISS HESSEL: Here he is.

JOHAN *enters right.*

BERNICK (*goes towards him*): Johan—!

JOHAN (*waves him aside*): First you listen to me. Yesterday morning I gave you my word to keep my mouth shut.

BERNICK: You did.

JOHAN: I didn't know then that—

BERNICK: Johan, just let me briefly explain the circumstances—

JOHAN: There's no need; I know all about the circumstances. The firm was in difficulties; I'd left the country; you had a name and a reputation at stake. Oh, I don't blame you so much for that; we were young and reckless in those days. But now the truth will have to be revealed. I need it.

BERNICK: I can't reveal the truth just now. I need all the moral credit I can muster.

JOHAN: I don't mind about the lies you've been spreading about me. It's this business with Dina's mother. You've got to admit it was you. Dina's going to become my wife, and I want to live with her here, and build a new life with her here, in this town.

MISS HESSEL: You want to do that?

BERNICK: With Dina? As your wife? Here?

JOHAN: Yes, here. I want to stay here to silence all these liars and scandalmongers. But she won't marry me unless you clear my name.

BERNICK: Don't you realize that if I admit to the one I'm automatically confessing to the other? You think I only

79

need to show the firm's books to prove nothing was stolen? But I can't do that—our books weren't kept very carefully in those days. And even if I could, what good would it do? I'd stand revealed as a man who'd saved his skin by telling a lie, and had allowed this lie with all its consequences to be believed for fifteen years without raising a finger to contradict it. You don't know this community as well as you used to, or you'd realize that to do this would ruin me completely.

JOHAN: All I can say is that I intend to make Mrs Dorf's daughter my wife and live with her here in this town.

BERNICK (*wipes the sweat from his forehead*): Listen, Johan— and you too, Lona. I'm in a very particular position just now. If you do this to me you'll destroy me, and not only me but a future of great prosperity and happiness for the community which nurtured you.

JOHAN: And if I don't I shall destroy my own chances of happiness for ever.

MISS HESSEL: Go on, Karsten.

BERNICK: Now listen. It's to do with this question of the railway, and that isn't such a simple matter as you may think. I suppose you've heard there was talk last year about building a coast line? A good many influential voices were raised in support of it, both here and elsewhere in the neighbourhood, especially in the press; but I managed to stop it, because it would have damaged our steamship trade along the coast.

MISS HESSEL: Have you an interest in this steamship trade?

BERNICK: Yes. But no one dared to suspect me of acting from that motive. My name and my reputation forbade that. In any case, I could have carried the loss; but the town couldn't have. So they decided to run the line inland. Once this had been decided I secretly took steps to assure myself that it would be practicable for a branch line to be extended here.

MISS HESSEL: Why secretly, Karsten?

BERNICK: Have you heard about the big purchases that have been made of forests and mines and waterfalls—?

80

MISS HESSEL: Yes, by a syndicate from one of the other towns.

BERNICK: Under present conditions these properties are virtually worthless to their various owners, so they went comparatively cheaply. If one had waited till the project of the branch line had been made public, the prices of these properties would have rocketed exorbitantly.

MISS HESSEL: Yes, well; what of it?

BERNICK: Now we come to something that could bear two different interpretations—something that a member of our community could only admit to if his name and reputation were such as to set him above suspicion.

MISS HESSEL: Yes?

BERNICK: It was I who bought all those properties.

MISS HESSEL: You?

JOHAN: On your own?

BERNICK: On my own. If the branch line gets built, I am a millionaire. If it doesn't get built, I am ruined.

MISS HESSEL: That was a big risk, Karsten.

BERNICK: I have risked all the money I possess.

MISS HESSEL: I'm not thinking of your money. When it gets known that—

BERNICK: Yes, that's the point. With the reputation I have now I can accept the responsibility for this act, carry it through to its conclusion and say to my fellow citizens: "Look! I have taken this risk for the sake of the community."

MISS HESSEL: Of the community?

BERNICK: Yes. And no one will question my motive.

MISS HESSEL: But there are others here who've acted more openly than you, and with no ulterior motive.

BERNICK: Who?

MISS HESSEL: Rummel, Sandstad and Vigeland, of course.

BERNICK: In order to win their support I was compelled to take them into my confidence.

MISS HESSEL: Oh?

BERNICK: They demanded a fifth of the profits, to be shared amongst them.

MISS HESSEL: Oh, these pillars of society!

BERNICK: Doesn't society itself force us to use these backstairs methods? What would have happened if I hadn't acted secretly? Everyone would have charged in, they'd have divided and dispersed the properties and bungled and wrecked the whole enterprise. There isn't one man in this town apart from me who understands how to organize a project of this magnitude. Up here, it's only the families who have migrated from the cities who have any talent for big business. That's why my conscience tells me I have acted correctly in this matter. Only in my hands can these properties be of any permanent value to the thousands of people whom I intend that they shall benefit.

MISS HESSEL: I think you're right there, Karsten.

JOHAN: But I don't know these thousands of people, and my life and my happiness are at stake.

BERNICK: The prosperity of your birthplace is also at stake. If anything comes to light which casts a shadow on my early career, all my enemies will unite to destroy me. A youthful indiscretion won't be forgiven in this community. People will examine my whole life under a microscope, dig up a hundred trivial incidents and reinterpret them in the light of this revelation. They will destroy me with their rumours and innuendoes. I shall have to withdraw from the railway project; and if I do that, it will fail, and I shall be ruined and ostracized.

MISS HESSEL: Johan, after what you've just heard you must go away and keep your mouth shut.

BERNICK: Yes, yes, Johan, you must!

JOHAN: All right. I'll go. And I'll keep my mouth shut. But I shall come back, and when I do I shall speak.

BERNICK: Stay over there, Johan. Keep quiet about this, and I'll gladly give you a share of—

JOHAN: Keep your money. Give me back my name and my honour.

BERNICK: And sacrifice my own?

JOHAN: You and your community must work that out between you. I want to marry Dina; I must and shall marry her. So I'm leaving tomorrow. In the *Indian Girl*—

BERNICK: The *Indian Girl*?

JOHAN: Yes. The captain's promised to take me with him. I'm going back to America, to sell my ranch and put my affairs in order. In two months I shall be here again.

BERNICK: And then you'll talk?

JOHAN: Then the guilty will have to pay for his crime.

BERNICK: Are you forgetting that I shall also have to pay for a crime of which I am not guilty?

JOHAN: Who was it who profited by the false rumour of fifteen years ago?

BERNICK: You're making me desperate. If you speak, I shall deny everything. I shall say there's a conspiracy against me; a plot for revenge. I shall say you have come here to blackmail me.

MISS HESSEL: Karsten!

BERNICK: I'm desperate, I tell you; and I'm fighting for my life. I shall deny everything, everything!

JOHAN: I have your two letters. I found them in my trunk with my other papers. I read them again this morning. They're plain enough.

BERNICK: And you intend to publish them?

JOHAN: If you force me to.

BERNICK: And in two months you say you will be back?

JOHAN: I hope so. The winds are favourable. In three weeks I shall be in New York—if the *Indian Girl* doesn't sink—

BERNICK (*starts*): Sink? Why should the *Indian Girl* sink?

JOHAN: No, why should she?

BERNICK (*scarcely audibly*): Sink?

JOHAN: Well, Bernick, now you know how things are. You'd better start thinking. Goodbye. You can give my love to Betty, though she's hardly received me in a very sisterly manner. But I want to see Martha. She must tell Dina—she must promise me—

He goes out through the door upstage left.

BERNICK (*to himself*): The *Indian Girl*? (*Quickly*) Lona, you must stop him!

MISS HESSEL: You can see for yourself, Karsten. I haven't any power over him any longer.

83

She follows JOHAN *into the room left.*

BERNICK (*ponders uneasily*): Sink?

AUNE *enters right.*

AUNE: Excuse me, Mr Bernick. Can you spare me a moment?

BERNICK (*turns angrily*): What do you want?

AUNE: I'd like permission to ask you a question.

BERNICK: All right, but be quick. What is it?

AUNE: I wanted to ask if you're still resolved to dismiss me if the *Indian Girl* doesn't sail tomorrow?

BERNICK: Why ask me that? She'll be ready now, won't she?

AUNE: She'll be ready. But if she wasn't, it'd mean my dismissal?

BERNICK: Why are you asking me these foolish questions?

AUNE: I'd like to know, Mr Bernick. Answer me; would it mean my dismissal?

BERNICK: Do I usually stand by my word?

AUNE: Then tomorrow I'd lose my position in my home, and among the people I belong to. I'd lose my influence among the workmen; lose my chance to do anything for the poor and humble of this community.

BERNICK: Aune, we've discussed all that.

AUNE: Right, then the *Indian Girl* can sail.

Short silence.

BERNICK: Look, I can't have eyes everywhere; I can't be personally responsible for everything. You give me your promise, don't you, that the repairs have been executed satisfactorily?

AUNE: You didn't give me much time, Mr Bernick.

BERNICK: But the work has been done properly?

AUNE: The weather's good, and it's midsummer.

Another silence.

BERNICK: Have you anything else to say to me?

AUNE: I don't know of anything else, Mr Bernick.

BERNICK: Then—the *Indian Girl* will sail—

AUNE: Tomorrow?
BERNICK: Yes.
AUNE: Very good.

Touches his forehead and goes. BERNICK *stands for a moment, torn by doubt; then he strides quickly over to the door as though to call* AUNE *back, but stops uneasily with his hand on the door-handle. As he does so, the door is opened from the outside and* KRAP *enters.*

KRAP (*quietly*): Oh, so he's been here. Has he confessed?
BERNICK: Hm—did you discover anything?
KRAP: What's the need? Couldn't you see from his eyes that he had a bad conscience?
BERNICK: Oh, nonsense, one can't *see* things like that. I asked you if you discovered anything.
KRAP: Couldn't get to her. Too late; they'd already started hauling her out of the dock. But the very fact that they were in such a hurry proves—
BERNICK: It proves nothing. They've completed the inspection, then?
KRAP: Of course, but—
BERNICK: There, you see! And they've found nothing to complain of. ·
KRAP: Mr Bernick, you know what these inspections are, especially in a yard with a reputation like ours.
BERNICK: Nevertheless, it means that no blame can be attached to us.
KRAP: But, Mr Bernick, surely you could see from the way Aune—
BERNICK: Aune has convinced me that there is nothing to fear.
KRAP: And I tell you I'm morally convinced that—
BERNICK: Look here, Krap, what the devil are you getting at? I know you've a grudge against this man, but if you want to pick a quarrel with him you'll have to find other grounds than this. You know how vitally important it is for me—for the company—that the *Indian Girl* sails tomorrow.
KRAP: All right. Let her sail. But how far she'll go—hm!

85

VIGELAND: Good morning, Mr Bernick, good morning! Can you spare me a moment?

BERNICK: Yes, of course, Mr Vigeland.

VIGELAND: I just wanted to ask if you agree that the *Palm Tree* shall sail tomorrow.

BERNICK: Why, yes. It's all settled.

VIGELAND: Only that the captain came just now to tell me there's a gale warning.

KRAP: The barometer's fallen heavily since this morning.

BERNICK: Oh? Do they expect a storm?

VIGELAND: Well, a stiff breeze. But no head wind; on the contrary—

BERNICK: Hm. Well, what do you say?

VIGELAND: I say, as I said to the captain: "The *Palm Tree* rests in the hand of Providence." Besides, she's only got the North Sea to cross on her first leg; and freight charges are pretty high in England just now, so—

BERNICK: Yes, it'd certainly be expensive to delay her.

VIGELAND: She's solidly built; and anyway, she's fully insured. She's a good risk; not like that *Indian Girl*—

BERNICK: What do you mean?

VIGELAND: She's sailing tomorrow, too.

BERNICK: Yes, we've worked overtime on her; besides—

VIGELAND: Well, if that old coffin can sail—especially with the crew she's got—it'd be a poor thing if we were afraid to—

BERNICK: Quite, quite. You have the ship's papers with you?

VIGELAND: Yes, here.

BERNICK: Good. Mr Krap, will you see to them?

KRAP: This way, Mr Vigeland. We'll soon get this settled.

VIGELAND: Thank you. And the outcome, Mr Bernick, we leave in the hands of the Almighty.

He goes with KRAP *into the room downstage left.* ROERLUND *enters through the garden.*

ROERLUND: Why, fancy seeing you here at this time of day, Mr Bernick.

BERNICK (*abstractedly*): Mm?

ROERLUND: I really came to speak to your wife. I thought she might need a few words of consolation.

BERNICK: I'm sure she does. But I'd like to have a word with you too.

ROERLUND: With pleasure, Mr Bernick. Is something the matter? You look quite pale and upset.

BERNICK: Oh? Do I? Well, what can you expect with everything piling up on me the way it has these last few days? I've got my own business to look after without this railway— Listen, Dr Roerlund: tell me something. Let me ask you a question.

ROERLUND: By all means, Mr Bernick.

BERNICK: It's just a thought that occurred to me. When a man stands on the threshold of a great and ambitious enterprise which has as its object the creation of prosperity for thousands of people—suppose this enterprise should claim one, just one victim—?

ROERLUND: How do you mean?

BERNICK: Well, say a man is thinking of building a great factory. He knows for certain, because all his experience has taught him, that sooner or later in this factory human life will be lost.

ROERLUND: Yes, I fear that is only too likely.

BERNICK: Or a man is planning to open a mine. He employs men with children, and young men with all their lives before them. It's certain, is it not, that some of these men will lose their lives in his service?

ROERLUND: Alas, yes.

BERNICK: Well. A man in such a position knows before he starts that the project he is launching will at some stage of its development cost human life. But this project is for the general good. For every life it takes it will, equally beyond doubt, provide the means of happiness for many hundreds of people.

ROERLUND: Ah, you're thinking of the railway—all that dangerous quarrying and dynamiting and so on—

BERNICK: Yes, yes, exactly. I'm thinking of the railway. And

87

the railway will mean mines and factories— Remembering all this, do you still feel— ?

ROERLUND: My dear Mr Bernick, your conscience is too tender. I believe that as long as one entrusts one's work to the hands of Providence—

BERNICK: Yes; yes, of course; Providence—

ROERLUND: —one is absolved from guilt. Build your railway, and have no fear.

BERNICK: Yes, but now I want to give you a particular example. Suppose a mountainside has to be blasted at a dangerous spot; and if this isn't done, the railway cannot be completed. I know, and the engineer knows, that it will cost the life of the man who lights the fuse; but it must be lit, and it is the engineer's duty to send a man to do it.

ROERLUND: Hm—

BERNICK: I know what you're going to say. The engineer ought to take the match and go himself to light the fuse. But such things aren't done. He must sacrifice one of his men.

ROERLUND: No engineer in this country would do it.

BERNICK: No engineer in a big country would think twice about doing it.

ROERLUND: Yes, I can quite believe that. In those depraved and unscrupulous societies—

BERNICK: Oh, there's some merit in those societies—

ROERLUND: How can you say that? Why, you yourself—

BERNICK: In big countries men at least have elbow-room to plan ambitiously for the general good. They have courage to make sacrifices for the sake of a cause; but here one's hands are tied by all kinds of petty scruples and considerations.

ROERLUND: Is a human life a petty consideration?

BERNICK: When it's weighed against the general good, yes.

ROERLUND: But the examples you suggest are quite unrealistic, Mr Bernick. I really can't make you out today. These great communities you speak of—what is a human life worth there? They think of human life simply as capital. Our ethical standpoint is completely different. Look at our

88

great shipyards! Name one shipowner in this town who would think of sacrificing a human life for mercenary motives! And then think of those scoundrels in your great communities who, to increase their profits, send out one unseaworthy ship after another—

BERNICK: I'm not talking about unseaworthy ships!

ROERLUND: But I am talking about them, Mr Bernick.

BERNICK: Why bring that up? That's got nothing to do with it. Oh, this wretched narrowness and timidity! If a general in this country sent his men into battle and saw them shot down, he'd have sleepless nights. It isn't so in big countries. You should hear that fellow in there talking about—

ROERLUND: What fellow? The American?

BERNICK: Yes. You should hear him describe how people in America—

ROERLUND: Is he in there? Why didn't you tell me? I'll soon see to him—

BERNICK: Oh, it's no use. You won't get anywhere with him.

ROERLUND: We'll see about that. Ah, here he is.

JOHAN TOENNESEN *enters from the room on the left.*

JOHAN (*talks back through the open door*): All right, Dina, as you wish. But I'm not giving you up. I'm coming back, and when I do everything's going to be all right.

ROERLUND: May I ask what you mean by those words? What exactly do you want?

JOHAN: That young girl, before whom you slandered me yesterday, is going to be my wife.

ROERLUND: *Your*—? Do you really imagine that—?

JOHAN: I want her as my wife.

ROERLUND: Very well. I suppose you'll have to be told. (*Goes across to the door, which is still ajar*) Mrs Bernick, will you please come and witness this? You too, Miss Martha. And let Dina come too. (*Sees* MISS HESSEL) Oh. Are you here?

MISS HESSEL (*in the doorway*): Can I come too?

ROERLUND: By all means. The more the better.

BERNICK: What are you going to do?

89

MISS HESSEL, MRS BERNICK, MARTHA, DINA *and* HILMAR
enter from the room.

MRS BERNICK: Oh, Dr Roerlund, I tried to stop him, but—

ROERLUND: I shall stop him, Mrs Bernick. Dina, you are a
rash and thoughtless girl. But I do not reproach you. For
too long you have lacked the moral support which you so
grievously need. I reproach myself for not having provided
you with that support earlier.

DINA: You mustn't tell them now!

MRS BERNICK: What is all this?

ROERLUND: I must tell them now, Dina, although your conduct yesterday and today has made it ten times more
difficult for me. But you must be saved, and all other considerations must yield to that. You remember the promise I
made you, and the answer you promised to give me when I
should decide that the time had come. Now I dare delay no
longer; therefore— (*To* JOHAN) This young girl after whom
you lust is betrothed to me.

MRS BERNICK: What!

BERNICK: Dina!

JOHAN: She? To you?

MARTHA: No, Dina, no!

MISS HESSEL: It's a lie!

JOHAN: Dina. Is that man speaking the truth?

DINA (*after a brief pause*): Yes.

ROERLUND: Let us pray that by this the arts of the seducer
will be rendered powerless. This decision, which I have
resolved to take in order to secure Dina's happiness, may be
revealed to the rest of our community; I raise no objection.
I sincerely trust it will not be misinterpreted. Meanwhile,
Mrs Bernick, I think it would be wisest to remove her to
her room and to try to restore her calm and equilibrium.

MRS BERNICK: Yes, come with me. Oh, Dina, what a lucky
girl you are!

She leads DINA *out, left.* DR ROERLUND *goes with them.*

MARTHA: Goodbye, Johan.

She goes.

HILMAR (*in the verandah doorway*): Hm. Well, really! I must say—!

MISS HESSEL (*who has watched* DINA *go out; to* JOHAN): Don't lose heart, son. I'll stay here to keep an eye on the Reverend.

She goes out right.

BERNICK: Well, Johan, this means you won't be sailing in the *Indian Girl*.

JOHAN: It means I shall.

BERNICK: But you won't be coming back?

JOHAN: I'll come back.

BERNICK: After this? But what can you want here now?

JOHAN: To take my revenge on you all. To break as many of you as I can.

He goes out right. VIGELAND *and* KRAP *enter from* BERNICK'S *office.*

VIGELAND: Well, all the papers are in order now, Mr Bernick.

BERNICK: Good, good.

KRAP (*whispers*): You still want the *Indian Girl* to sail to-morrow, then?

BERNICK: Yes.

He goes into his office. VIGELAND *and* KRAP *go out right.* HILMAR *is about to follow them when* OLAF *pokes his head cautiously out of the doorway to the room left.*

OLAF: Uncle! Uncle Hilmar!

HILMAR: Ugh, is it you? Why aren't you upstairs? You're under house arrest.

OLAF (*takes a step towards him*): Ssh! Uncle Hilmar, have you heard the news?

HILMAR: Yes, I hear you've had a hiding today.

OLAF (*scowls towards his father's office*): He won't hit me again. But have you heard that Uncle Johan's sailing to America tomorrow?

91

HILMAR: What's that to do with you? Now you run upstairs again.

OLAF: I'll fight those redskins yet.

HILMAR: Oh, stuff! A little coward like you?

OLAF: Just you wait till tomorrow. You'll see.

HILMAR: Jackass!

He goes out through the garden. OLAF *runs back into the room and shuts the door as he sees* KRAP *enter right.*

KRAP (*goes over to* BERNICK'S *door and half-opens it*): Excuse me disturbing you again, Mr Bernick, but there's a dreadful storm blowing up. (*Waits for a moment; there is no reply*) Shall the *Indian Girl* sail?

Short pause.

BERNICK (*from his room*): The *Indian Girl* shall sail.

KRAP *closes the door and goes out right.*

ACT FOUR

The same. The work-table has been moved out. It is a stormy afternoon, already twilight; during the scene it grows gradually darker. A FOOTMAN *lights the chandelier. Two* MAIDS *bring in pots of flowers, lamps and candles, and place them on the tables and in brackets on the walls.* RUMMEL, *in tails, with gloves and a white cravat, is standing in the room giving orders.*

RUMMEL (*to the* FOOTMAN): Only every second candle, Jacob. We mustn't look too festive; it's meant to be a surprise. Oh, and all these flowers—? Ah, well, let them stay. People will think they're always here—

> BERNICK *enters from his office.*

BERNICK (*in the doorway*): What's the meaning of all this?
RUMMEL: Oh dear, you weren't meant to see. (*To the* SERVANTS) All right, you can go now.

The FOOTMAN *and* MAIDS *go out through the door upstage left.*

BERNICK (*comes closer*): Rummel, what on earth does all this mean?
RUMMEL: It means that your proudest moment has come. The whole town is marching here in procession this evening to pay homage to its foremost citizen.
BERNICK: What!
RUMMEL: With banners and a brass band. We were going to have torches, but the weather was so doubtful we didn't dare risk it. Still, there's to be an illumination. That'll look well in the newspapers.
BERNICK: Look, Rummel, I'd rather we didn't have this.
RUMMEL: Well, it's too late now. They'll be here in half an hour.

BERNICK: But why didn't you tell me about it before?

RUMMEL: I was afraid you might object to the idea. I had a word with your wife, and she gave me permission to make a few arrangements. She's looking after the refreshments herself.

BERNICK (*listens*): What's that? Are they coming already? I think I hear singing.

RUMMEL (*at the verandah door*): Singing? Oh, that's only the Americans. The *Indian Girl* is being hauled out to the buoy.

BERNICK: Is she hauling out? Yes. No, I can't this evening, Rummel. I'm not feeling well.

RUMMEL: Yes, you look off-colour. But you must pull yourself together. Damn it, man, you must! I and Sandstad and Vigeland attach the utmost importance to this ceremony. So spectacular a display of public feeling will completely crush our opponents. Rumours are spreading in the town; the news of the property deals is bound to come out soon. You must let them know this evening, against a background of songs and speeches, and the merry clink of glasses—in short, in an atmosphere of holiday and carnival—how much you have staked for the welfare of the community. In such an atmosphere of holiday and carnival, as I have just phrased it, we can get the hell of a lot done. But we've got to have that atmosphere, or it'll be no good.

BERNICK: Yes, yes, yes—

RUMMEL: Especially when the issue is such a delicate and ticklish one. Thank heaven you've the name and reputation you have, Bernick. But listen, now. I must tell you about the arrangements. Hilmar Toennesen has written a song in your honour. It's very beautiful; it begins: "Wave high the banner of ideals!" And Dr Roerlund is to make the speech. You'll have to reply, of course.

BERNICK: I can't do that this evening, Rummel. Couldn't you—?

RUMMEL: Impossible! Much as I'd like to. The speech will naturally be addressed mainly to you. Possibly just a word or two about us too. I've been discussing it with Vigeland

and Sandstad. We thought you might reply with a toast to the prosperity of the community. Sandstad will say something about the harmony that exists between the various strata of our society; Vigeland will want to stress how important it is that this new enterprise should not disturb the moral foundations on which our life is so firmly based; and I'm thinking of paying a brief tribute to the ladies, whose contribution to the welfare of our community, while humble and unassuming, must not be overlooked. But you're not listening.

BERNICK: Yes, yes, I am. But tell me—is the sea very rough this evening?

RUMMEL: Are you worrying about the *Palm Tree*? She's well insured.

BERNICK: Insured, yes. But—

RUMMEL: And in good trim. That's the main thing.

BERNICK: Hm. If anything should happen to a ship, it doesn't necessarily follow that human lives will be lost. The ship and her cargo, perhaps—chests and papers—

RUMMEL: Damn, it man, chests and papers aren't that important.

BERNICK: Of course not. No, no—I only meant— Quiet! They're singing again.

RUMMEL: That'll be the crew of the *Palm Tree*.

VIGELAND *enters right.*

VIGELAND: Well, the *Palm Tree*'s hauling out now. Good evening, Mr Bernick.

BERNICK: You're a seaman. Do you still feel confident that—?

VIGELAND: Providence will decide, Mr Bernick; of that I am confident. Besides, I've been on board myself and distributed a few little tracts which I trust will ensure God's blessing on her.

SANDSTAD *and* KRAP *enter right.*

SANDSTAD (*still in the doorway*): Well, if that ship survives, I'll believe in miracles. Oh—good evening, good evening!

BERNICK: Anything wrong, Mr Krap?

KRAP: I said nothing, Mr Bernick.

SANDSTAD: The whole crew of the *Indian Girl* is drunk. If those brutes get that ship safely across the Atlantic, I'm a Dutchman.

MISS HESSEL *enters right.*

MISS HESSEL (*to* BERNICK): He asked me to say goodbye to you.

BERNICK: Is he aboard already?

MISS HESSEL: He will be any moment. I left him outside the hotel.

BERNICK: And he's still determined—?

MISS HESSEL: Absolutely determined.

RUMMEL (*over by the windows*): Confound these new-fangled contraptions. I can't get these curtains down.

MISS HESSEL: You want them down? I thought they were to stay up.

RUMMEL: Down to begin with, madam. I suppose you know what's going to happen?

MISS HESSEL: Yes, I know. Let me help you. (*Takes the cords*) Yes, I'll lower the curtain on my brother-in-law; though I'd sooner lift it.

RUMMEL: You can do that later. When the garden is filled with the surging throng, the curtains will be raised to reveal an amazed and happy family circle. A citizen's home should be as a house of glass, open to the gaze of all.

BERNICK *seems about to speak, but turns quickly and goes into his room.*

RUMMEL: Well, let's just run through the arrangements. Come along, Mr Krap. We need your help on a few details.

All the GENTLEMEN *go into* BERNICK'S *room.* MISS HESSEL *has drawn the curtains over the windows and is just about to do the same across the open glass door when* OLAF *jumps down on to the verandah from above. He has a plaid over his shoulder and a bundle in his hand.*

MISS HESSEL: Oh, my goodness, Olaf, how you frightened me!

OLAF (*hiding his bundle*): Ssh!

MISS HESSEL: Did you jump out of that window? Where are you going?

OLAF: Ssh! Don't tell anyone! I'm going to Uncle Johan. Only down to the jetty, of course—just to say goodbye to him. Good night, Aunt Lona!

He runs out through the garden.

MISS HESSEL: No, wait! Olaf, Olaf!

JOHAN TOENNESEN, *in travelling clothes, with a bag over his shoulder, enters cautiously right.*

JOHAN: Lona!

MISS HESSEL (*turns*): What! Are you here again?

JOHAN: I've still got a few minutes. I must see her just once more. We can't part like this.

MARTHA *and* DINA, *both wearing overcoats, and the latter with a small travelling-bag in her hand, enter through the door upstage left.*

DINA: I must see him, I must see him!

MARTHA: Yes, Dina. You'll see him.

DINA: There he is!

JOHAN: Dina!

DINA: Take me with you.

JOHAN: What?

MISS HESSEL: You want to go with him?

DINA: Yes! Take me with you! That man says he's going to make a public announcement this evening in front of the whole town about—

JOHAN: Dina! You don't love him?

DINA: I have never loved him. I'd die rather than be engaged to him. Oh, how he humiliated me yesterday with his fine phrases! He made me feel he was raising something contemptible up to his own level. I'm not going to be humiliated like that any more. I'm going away. Can I come with you?

JOHAN: Yes! Yes!

DINA: I shan't trouble you for long. Just help me to get over there; help me to find my feet—

JOHAN: Yippee! Don't you worry about that, Dina!

MISS HESSEL (*points towards* BERNICK'S *door*): Ssh! Quiet, quiet!

JOHAN: I'll take care of you, Dina!

DINA: No. I won't let you do that. I'm going to look after myself. I'll manage to do that over there. If only I can get away from here! Oh, these women—you've no idea! They've written to me today begging me to realize how lucky I am, and reminding me how noble and magnanimous he's been. Tomorrow and the next day and every day they'll be squinting at me to see whether I'm proving myself worthy of him. Oh, all this respectability frightens me so much!

JOHAN: Tell me, Dina. Is that the only reason you're leaving? Am I nothing to you?

DINA: Oh, no, Johan. You mean more to me than anyone else in the world.

JOHAN: Oh, Dina!

DINA: Everyone here tells me I ought to hate you and detest you. They say it's my duty. But I don't understand all this about duty. I never shall.

MISS HESSEL: That's right, child! Don't you!

MARTHA: Yes, Dina. Go with him. As his wife.

JOHAN: Yes! Yes!

MISS HESSEL: What? I'll have to kiss you for that, Martha. I hadn't expected that from you.

MARTHA: No, I suppose not. I hadn't expected it myself. But I've got to speak out some time. Oh, how we suffer here under this tyranny of duty and convention! Rebel against it, Dina! Marry him. Do something to defy all their stupid ideals!

JOHAN: What do you say, Dina?

DINA: Yes. I will be your wife.

JOHAN: Dina!

DINA: But first I want to work and become someone. The way you have. I don't just want to be something someone takes.

98

MISS HESSEL: Sensible girl! That's the way!

JOHAN: Right! I'll wait, and hope—

MISS HESSEL: You'll win her, son. But now it's time for you both to go aboard.

JOHAN: Yes—aboard! Oh, Lona, my dear sister! Here, I want a word with you—

He leads her upstage and whispers quickly to her.

MARTHA: Dina, my dear, let me look at you. Let me kiss you once again. For the last time.

DINA: Not for the last time. No, dear, dear Aunt Martha! We'll meet again!

MARTHA: No; we never shall. Promise me, Dina—don't ever come back. (*Clasps both* DINA'S *hands and looks at her*) Go, my dear child—go to your happiness across the sea. Oh, down in that schoolroom I've so often longed to be over there! It must be beautiful there. The sky is larger and the clouds fly higher than they do here. The air that blows on the faces of the people is freer—

DINA: Oh, Aunt Martha, you must come and join us. Some day.

MARTHA: I? Never; never. My little task lies here. Now I think I can resign myself to being what I must be.

DINA: I can't imagine being without you.

MARTHA: Oh, one can learn to manage without almost anything, Dina. (*Kisses her*) But you'll never have to test the truth of that, my dear. Promise me you'll make him happy.

DINA: I won't promise anything. I hate promises. What will be will be.

MARTHA: Yes, yes, my dear. Always be as you are now. Be true to yourself. And believe in yourself.

DINA: I will, Aunt Martha.

MISS HESSEL (*puts some papers which* JOHAN *has given her into her pocket*): Good boy, Johan. All right, I'll do that. But now be off with you!

JOHAN: Yes, we've no time to waste. Goodbye, Lona—thanks for everything you've done for me. Goodbye, Martha. Thank you too. You've been a wonderful friend.

MARTHA: Goodbye, Johan! Goodbye, Dina! God bless you and make you happy—always!

MARTHA *and* MISS HESSEL *hurry them to the verandah door.* JOHAN *and* DINA *run out through the garden.* MISS HESSEL *closes the door and draws the curtain over it.*

MISS HESSEL: Now we're alone, Martha. You've lost her, and I've lost him.

MARTHA: *You*'ve lost him?

MISS HESSEL: Oh, I'd half-lost him already over there. The boy wanted to stand on his own feet, so I pretended I was pining to come back here.

MARTHA: Was that why? Now I see why you came. But he wants you to go back and join them.

MISS HESSEL: An old half-sister? What good can she be to him now? Men destroy a lot of things to find happiness.

MARTHA: It happens sometimes.

MISS HESSEL: But we'll stick together, Martha.

MARTHA: Can I be of any use to you?

MISS HESSEL: Who better? We two foster-mothers—haven't we both lost our children? Now we're alone.

MARTHA: Yes; alone. You might as well know now. I loved him more than anything else in the world.

MISS HESSEL: Martha! (*Grips her arm*) Is this true?

MARTHA: That's been my life. I loved him, and waited for him. Every summer I waited for him to come through that door. At last he came; but he didn't see me.

MISS HESSEL: You loved him! But it was you yourself who put happiness into his hands.

MARTHA: What else should I have done, if I loved him? Yes, I loved him. I've only lived for him, ever since he went away. What ground did I have for hope, you're wondering? Oh, I thought I had a little. But then, when he came back, it was just as though everything had been wiped clean from his memory. He didn't see me.

MISS HESSEL: Because of Dina, Martha. You stood in her shadow.

MARTHA: I'm glad. When he left, we were the same age; but

when I saw him again—oh, that dreadful moment!—I suddenly realized that now I was ten years older than him. He'd been walking over there in the bright, quivering sunlight, drawing in youth and strength with every breath, while I'd been sitting in here, spinning and spinning—

MISS HESSEL: The thread of his happiness, Martha.

MARTHA: Yes, it was gold I was spinning. I mustn't be bitter. It's true, isn't it, Lona—we two have been good sisters to him?

MISS HESSEL (*throws her arms round her*): Martha!

BERNICK *enters from his room.*

BERNICK (*to the* GENTLEMEN *inside his room*): Yes, yes, yes, make what arrangements you please. I'll manage when the time comes— (*Closes the door*) Oh, are you here? Look, Martha, you'd better go and dress up a bit. And tell Betty to do the same. Nothing grand, of course. Just something neat and simple. You must be quick, though.

MISS HESSEL: And you must look happy and excited, Martha. This is a joyful occasion for us all.

BERNICK: Olaf must come down too. I want to have him by my side.

MISS HESSEL: Hm. Olaf—

MARTHA: I'll go and tell Betty.

She goes out through the door upstage left.

MISS HESSEL: Well. Now the great moment's arrived.

BERNICK (*paces uneasily up and down*): Yes, so it has.

MISS HESSEL: I imagine a man must feel very proud and happy at such a moment.

BERNICK (*looks at her*): Hm.

MISS HESSEL: The whole town's to be illuminated, I hear.

BERNICK: Yes, they've planned something of the kind.

MISS HESSEL: All the guilds are to march here with their banners. Your name is to shine in letters of fire. Tonight the news will be telegraphed to every corner of the land: "Surrounded by his happy family, Karsten Bernick was acclaimed by his fellow citizens as a pillar of society."

BERNICK: Yes, that's right. And they're going to give three cheers for me outside there, and the crowd will demand that I show myself in the doorway here, and I shall be forced to bow and make a speech of thanks.

MISS HESSEL: Forced?

BERNICK: Do you think I feel happy at this moment?

MISS HESSEL: No, I don't imagine you can feel all that happy.

BERNICK: You despise me, don't you, Lona?

MISS HESSEL: Not yet.

BERNICK: You've no right to do that. To despise me. Oh, Lona, you can't imagine how dreadfully alone I am in this narrow, stunted society—how, year by year, I've had to renounce my hopes of really fulfilling myself and becoming what I might and could have become. What have I accomplished? It seems a lot, but really it's nothing—a patchwork of trivialities. But they wouldn't tolerate anything else here, or anything bigger. If I tried to move a step outside their conception of right and wrong, my power would vanish. Do you know what we are, we whom they call the pillars of society? We are the instruments of society. Nothing more.

MISS HESSEL: Why have you only begun to realize this now?

BERNICK: Because I've been thinking a great deal lately—since you came back. Especially this evening. Oh, Lona, why didn't I appreciate you then for what you were?

MISS HESSEL: And if you had?

BERNICK: I'd never have let you go. And if I'd had you beside me, I wouldn't stand where I do today.

MISS HESSEL: What about Betty? Haven't you ever thought what she might have been to you?

BERNICK: I only know she hasn't been the wife I needed.

MISS HESSEL: Because you've never let her share your work with you, or tried to establish a free and truthful relationship with her. Because you've allowed her to spend her life reproaching herself for the disgrace to her family for which you yourself are responsible.

BERNICK: Yes, yes, yes. Lying and cheating—that's the cause of it all.

MISS HESSEL: Then why don't you start telling the truth?

BERNICK: Now? It's too late now, Lona.

MISS HESSEL: Tell me, Karsten. What satisfaction does all this lying and cheating bring you?

BERNICK: None. I shall be destroyed, like the whole of this rotten society. But a generation will grow up after us. It's my son I'm working for; it's for him that I'm doing all this. A time will come when society will be founded on honesty and truth, and then he will be able to live a happier life than his father has.

MISS HESSEL: With a lie as the cornerstone of his existence? Think what an inheritance you're leaving your son.

BERNICK (*in subdued despair*): I am leaving him an inheritance a thousand times worse than you know. But some time the curse must end. And yet—in spite of everything—(*Violently*) How could you do all this to me? Well, now it's happened. Now I must go on. I won't let you destroy me!

HILMAR TOENNESEN, *an open letter in his hand, hastens in right, confused.*

HILMAR: But this is utterly—! Betty, Betty!

BERNICK: What is it now? Have they come already?

HILMAR: No, no. I must speak to someone—

He goes out through the door upstage left.

MISS HESSEL: Karsten, you say we came here to destroy you. Then let me tell you the metal he's made of, this prodigal whom your virtuous community treated like a leper. He can manage without you now. He's gone.

BERNICK: But he's coming back.

MISS HESSEL: Johan will never come back. He's gone for ever, and Dina has gone with him.

BERNICK: Never come back? And Dina—gone with him?

MISS HESSEL: Yes, to become his wife. There's a slap in the face for your virtuous community! Reminds me of the day I gave you a— ah well!

BERNICK: Gone? She too? In the *Indian Girl*?

MISS HESSEL: No. He didn't dare to risk so precious a cargo

with that gang of ruffians. Johan and Dina have sailed in the *Palm Tree*.

BERNICK: Ah! Then it was all for nothing—! (*Goes quickly to the door of his room, flings it open and shouts*) Krap, stop the *Indian Girl*! She mustn't sail tonight!

KRAP (*from the other room*): The *Indian Girl* is already standing out to sea, Mr Bernick.

BERNICK (*closes the door and says dully*): Too late! And for nothing—!

MISS HESSEL: What do you mean?

BERNICK: Nothing, nothing. Get away from me—!

MISS HESSEL: Hm. Look here, Karsten. Johan told me to tell you that he's entrusted to me the keeping of his good name, which he once entrusted to you and which you robbed him of while he was away. Johan will keep his mouth shut. And I can do as I choose. Look. I have your two letters here in my hand.

BERNICK: You have them! And now—now you're going to—this evening—when the procession arrives—?

MISS HESSEL: I didn't come here to unmask you. I came to shake you from your sleep, so that you'd stand up and tell the truth. I have failed. Very well, then. Go on living your lie. Look. I'm tearing your two letters up. Take the pieces. Now you have them. There's no evidence against you now, Karsten. You've nothing left to fear. Be happy—if you can.

BERNICK (*a shiver runs through his whole body*): Lona, why didn't you do this before? Now it's too late. Now my whole life is ruined. After today, I can't go on living.

MISS HESSEL: What has happened?

BERNICK: Don't ask me. And yet—I must live! I shall live! For Olaf's sake! He'll make everything right—he'll atone for everything—!

MISS HESSEL: Karsten!

HILMAR TOENNESEN *hurries back.*

HILMAR: I can't find him. He's gone. Betty too.

BERNICK: What's the matter with you?

HILMAR: I daren't tell you.

BERNICK: What is it? You must tell me!

HILMAR: Very well. Olaf has run away. He's gone—in the *Indian Girl*.

BERNICK (*recoils*): Olaf! In the *Indian Girl*! No! No!

MISS HESSEL: Yes, it's true. Now I understand. I saw him jump out of the window.

BERNICK (*in the doorway to his room, cries desperately*): Krap, stop the *Indian Girl*! Stop her at all costs!

KRAP (*comes out*): Impossible, Mr Bernick. How can we?

BERNICK: We must stop her. Olaf is on board.

KRAP: What!

RUMMEL (*enters from* BERNICK's *room*): Olaf run away? Impossible!

SANDSTAD (*enters*): They'll send him back with the pilot, Mr Bernick.

HILMAR: No, no. He's left me a letter. (*Shows it*) He says he'll hide among the cargo until they've reached the open sea.

BERNICK: I shall never see him again.

RUMMEL: Oh, rubbish. She's a good, strong ship, newly repaired—

VIGELAND (*who has also come out*): In your own yard, Mr Bernick.

BERNICK: I shall never see him again, I tell you. I've lost him, Lona. No—I realize it now. He never belonged to me. (*Listens*) What's that?

RUMMEL: Music. The procession's arriving.

BERNICK: I can't receive anyone. I won't!

RUMMEL: What on earth do you mean? You must!

SANDSTAD: You must, Mr Bernick. Remember what you have at stake.

BERNICK: What does that matter now? Whom have I to work for now?

RUMMEL: What a question to ask! You have us. And the community.

VIGELAND: Of course!

SANDSTAD: And you surely haven't forgotten that we too—

MARTHA *enters through the door upstage left. The music can be faintly heard from far down the street.*

MARTHA: The procession's arriving. I can't find Betty anywhere. I can't think where she—

BERNICK: Can't find her! You see, Lona! In sorrow as in joy, I stand alone.

RUMMEL: Up with those curtains! Come and help me, Mr Krap. You too, Mr Sandstad. Most regrettable that the whole family isn't here. That's not at all according to programme.

The curtains are raised from the windows and the door. The whole street is illuminated. On the house opposite is a big transparency, bearing the inscription: "Long live Karsten Bernick, The Pillar of our Society!"

BERNICK (*recoils*): Take that away! I don't want to see it! Put it out, put it out!

RUMMEL: My dear fellow, have you taken leave of your senses?

MARTHA: What's the matter with him, Lona?

MISS HESSEL: Ssh!

Whispers to her.

BERNICK: Take away this nonsense, I tell you! Can't you see that all these lights are a mockery!

RUMMEL: Well, really!

BERNICK: Oh, how could you understand? But I—I—! These are torches to light the dead to their graves!

KRAP: Hm!

RUMMEL: Now look! You're making too much of this.

SANDSTAD: The boy'll just take a trip across the Atlantic, and then you'll have him back home again.

VIGELAND: Put your trust in the hand of the Almighty, Mr Bernick.

RUMMEL: That ship's not ready to sink yet.

KRAP: Hm.

RUMMEL: It's not as though she was one of these floating coffins they send out in foreign countries—

Mrs Bernick, *a big shawl over her head, enters from the verandah.*

Mrs Bernick: Karsten, Karsten, have you heard?

Bernick: Yes, I've heard. But you—you see nothing! You're his mother, why didn't you look after him?

Mrs Bernick: Karsten, listen—

Bernick: Why didn't you keep a watch on him? I've lost him! Give him back to me, if you can.

Mrs Bernick: Yes, I can. I have him safe.

Bernick: You have him?

The Others: Ah!

Hilmar: Yes, I thought as much.

Martha: You've got him back, Karsten!

Miss Hessel: Yes. Now you must win him too.

Bernick: You have him safe! Do you really mean it? Where is he?

Mrs Bernick: I shan't tell you until you've forgiven him.

Bernick: Forgiven—! But how did you find out—?

Mrs Bernick: Do you think a mother hasn't eyes? I was terrified you might find out. Those few words he let fall yesterday—then I found his room was empty and his clothes and rucksack missing—

Bernick: Yes, yes.

Mrs Bernick: So I ran down and got hold of Aune. We went out in his boat. The American ship was just getting ready to sail. Thank heaven, we got there in time—went aboard—had the ship searched—found him. Oh, Karsten, you mustn't punish him!

Bernick: Betty!

Mrs Bernick: Or Aune either!

Bernick: Aune? What do you know about him? Is the *Indian Girl* under sail again?

Mrs Bernick: No, that's just it—

Bernick: Speak, speak!

Mrs Bernick: Aune was as frightened as I was. It took a long time to search the ship—darkness was falling, the pilot began to complain—so Aune took his courage in his hands and told them in your name—

BERNICK: Yes?

MRS BERNICK: To hold the ship until morning.

KRAP: Hm.

BERNICK: Oh, what luck! What incredible luck!

MRS BERNICK: You aren't angry?

BERNICK: Oh, Betty, thank God, thank God!

RUMMEL: Come, man, you're being over-sensitive.

HILMAR: Yes, as soon as anyone's bold enough to risk a little skirmish with the elements—ugh!

KRAP (*by the windows*): The procession's just coming through the garden gate!

BERNICK: Let them come.

RUMMEL: The whole garden's filling with people.

SANDSTAD: The street's crammed too.

RUMMEL: The entire town's here, Bernick. This is really an inspiring moment.

VIGELAND: Let us accept it in a humble spirit, Mr Bernick.

RUMMEL: All the flags are out. What a procession! There's the festival committee, with Dr Roerlund at its head.

BERNICK: Let them come, I say!

RUMMEL: Look; you're in a rather disturbed state of mind just now—

BERNICK: So?

RUMMEL: Well, if you don't feel up to it, I wouldn't mind saying a few words on your behalf.

BERNICK: No, thank you. This evening I shall speak for myself.

RUMMEL: But do you know what you have to say?

BERNICK: Yes, Rummel. Don't worry. I know what I have to say.

The music has ceased. The verandah door is thrown open. DR ROERLUND *enters at the head of the festival committee, accompanied by two* FOOTMEN *carrying a covered basket. After them come* CITIZENS *of all classes, as many as the room will hold. A huge crowd, with banners and flags, can be glimpsed outside in the garden and the street.*

ROERLUND: Most honoured sir! I see by the amazement on your face that our intrusion into this happy family circle, where you sit gathered at your peaceful fireside surrounded by active and honourable fellow citizens, takes you completely by surprise. But our hearts commanded that we should come and pay you homage. It is not the first time we have done this, but it is the first time we have done so on such a comprehensive scale. We have often expressed to you our thanks for the solid moral foundation on which you have, as one might say, grounded our community. But tonight we hail you as the far-sighted, indefatigable and selfless—nay, self-sacrificing—fellow citizen who has seized the initiative in launching an enterprise which, so expert opinion assures us, will give a powerful impetus to the material welfare and prosperity of our community.

VOICES FROM THE CROWD: Bravo, bravo!

ROERLUND: Mr Bernick, you have for many years been a shining example to our town. I am speaking now not of your model family life, nor of your untarnished moral record. These are matters for private admiration rather than public acclaim. I speak rather of your work as a citizen, which is apparent for all to see. Stately ships sail forth from your shipyards and show our country's flag upon the furthest corners of the globe. A numerous and contented family of workers reveres you as a father. By calling into existence new branches of industry you have given prosperity to hundreds of homes. You are, in a word, the cornerstone of our community.

VOICES: Hear, hear! Bravo!

ROERLUND: But what we especially bless in you is the shining altruism which irradiates your every action—a rare quality indeed in this modern age. You are now in the process of procuring for the community a—I do not flinch from the plain, prosaic word—a railway. *Applause*

MANY VOICES: Bravo, bravo!

ROERLUND: But this enterprise is threatened by obstacles deliberately placed in its path by narrow and selfish interests. *Yes. That's true*

VOICES: Hear, hear!

ROERLUND: It is not unknown that certain individuals who do not belong to our community have stolen a march on our own industrious citizens, and have secured certain advantages which rightly belonged to this town.

VOICES: Yes, yes. Hear, hear! *Shame*

ROERLUND: This regrettable information has, sir, doubtless come to your knowledge. None the less you are pursuing your project inflexibly, knowing that a true patriot's vision cannot be confined by the needs of his own parish.

VARIOUS VOICES: Hm. No, no! Yes, yes!

ROERLUND: It is therefore to the patriot and, in the largest sense, the model citizen, that we are gathered here tonight to pay homage. May God grant that your enterprise may result in true and lasting prosperity for this community! The railway is a road which may expose us to corrupting influences from without, but it will also be a road by which we shall swiftly be able to rid ourselves of them. We can, alas, no longer hope to isolate ourselves completely from the evil of the outside world. But the fact that on this evening of rejoicing we have, so it is rumoured, been rid with unexpected speed of one such influence—

VOICES: Ssh! Ssh!

ROERLUND: —I take as a happy omen for this enterprise. I only mention this as evidence that we stand here in a house in which ethical considerations carry greater weight than the ties of blood.

VOICES: Hear, hear! Bravo!

BERNICK (*simultaneously*): Allow me to—

ROERLUND: One word more, sir. What you have done for this parish you have, of course, done with no ulterior motive or thought of material advantage. But we trust you will not refuse to accept a small token of appreciation from your fellow citizens, least of all at this significant moment when, so men of practical experience assure us, we stand on the threshold of a new era.

MANY VOICES: Bravo! Hear, hear! *Applause*
Ladies — *Ssh. Ssh.*

He nods to the FOOTMEN, *who bring the basket closer. During the following, members of the Committee take out and present the objects described.*

ROERLUND: We therefore have the honour, Mr Bernick, to present you with this silver coffee-service. May it adorn your table when, in the days to come, as so often in days gone by, we shall enjoy the pleasure of gathering at your hospitable board. And you too, gentlemen, who have so steadfastly supported our foremost citizen, we beg to accept these small tokens of our affection. To you, Mr Rummel, this silver cup. You have often, in well-winged words, amid the clinking of cups, championed the civic interests of this community. May you often find worthy opportunities for raising and emptying this cup. To you, Mr Sandstad, I present this album containing photographs of your fellow citizens. Your famed and acknowledged generosity places you in the agreeable position of numbering friends in every stratum of the community, regardless of political differences. And to you, Mr Vigeland, to adorn your bedside, I offer this book of sermons, printed on vellum, and luxuriously bound. Under the ripening influence of the years you have arrived at a mature wisdom; your interest in temporal matters has been purified and sublimated by reflection upon loftier and less worldly things. (*Turns to the* CROWD) And now, my friends, three cheers for Mr Bernick and his fellows in the fight! Three cheers for the pillars of our society!

WHOLE CROWD: Long live Mr Bernick! Long live the pillars of our society! Hurrah! Hurrah! Hurrah!

MISS HESSEL: Good luck, brother-in-law.

An expectant silence.

BERNICK (*begins slowly and earnestly*): Fellow citizens! Your Chairman has said that we stand this evening on the threshold of a new era; and I hope this will prove to be the case. But for this to happen, we must face the truth, which until this evening has been an outcast from this community.

(*General amazement*) I must therefore begin by rejecting the words of praise with which you, Dr Roerlund, as is the custom on such occasions, addressed me. I am unworthy of them, for until today I have not acted selflessly. If I have not always acted from pecuniary motives, I none the less now realize that a desire for power, for influence and for reputation, has been the driving force behind most of my actions.

RUMMEL (*aside*): What's this?

BERNICK: However, I do not therefore reproach myself before my fellow citizens. For I still believe that I can be reckoned among the most useful of us who stand here tonight.

MANY VOICES: Hear, hear! Yes, yes!

BERNICK: I condemn myself most for having so often been weak enough to use backstairs methods, because I knew and feared our community's fondness for scenting impure motives behind everything a man does here. And that brings me to a case in point.

RUMMEL (*uneasily*): Hm-hm!

BERNICK: Rumours have been spreading about the big purchases of land that have been made in the neighbourhood. All these purchases have been made by me, and by me alone.

VOICES (*whisper*): What did he say? Him? Mr Bernick?

BERNICK: All that land belongs, at this moment, to me. I have of course confided this information to my partners in this enterprise, Messrs Rummel, Vigeland and Sandstad, and we have agreed that—

RUMMEL: It isn't true! Where's the proof? Show us the proof!

VIGELAND: We agreed nothing!

SANDSTAD: Well, I must say!

BERNICK: That is quite correct; we have not yet agreed on what I was about to propose. But I am confident that these three gentlemen will agree with me now when I say that I have this evening convinced myself that these properties should be turned into a public company, so that any citizen who wishes may buy a share in them.

MANY VOICES: Hurrah! Long live Mr Bernick!

RUMMEL (*quietly to* BERNICK): You damned traitor!

SANDSTAD (*also quietly*): You've cheated us!

VIGELAND: May the devil—oh, good heavens, what am I saying?

CROWD (*outside*): Hurrah, hurrah, hurrah!

BERNICK: Quiet, gentlemen! I am unworthy of this applause, for the decision I have now reached is not what I originally intended. I intended to keep all the land for myself, and I still believe that these properties can be best exploited if they come under the control of a single hand. But that is for you to decide. If it is the general wish, I am willing to administer them to the best of my ability.

VOICES: Yes! Yes! Yes!

BERNICK: But first my fellow citizens must know me as I really am. Let each man look into his own heart, and let us resolve that from tonight we shall in fact enter upon a new era. Let the old life, with its painted façade, its hypocrisy and its hollowness, its sham propriety and its miserable prejudices, survive only as a museum. And to this museum we shall give—shall we not, gentlemen?—our coffee-service, our silver cup, our photograph album and our book of sermons printed on vellum and luxuriously bound.

RUMMEL: Yes, of course.

VIGELAND (*mutters*): You've taken all the rest from us, so why not this?

SANDSTAD: Yes, yes.

BERNICK: And now to the chief issue that remains between me and my community. You have heard it asserted that evil influences have left us this evening. To that piece of news I can add another. The man in question did not leave alone. A girl went with him, to become his wife—

MISS HESSEL (*loudly*): Dina Dorf!

ROERLUND: What?

MRS BERNICK: Lona!

Great excitement.

ROERLUND: Fled? Run away—with him? Impossible!

BERNICK: To become his wife, Dr Roerlund. And I will tell you something else. (*Quietly*) Prepare yourself, Betty, for what I am about to say. (*Loudly*) I say: "Hats off to that man, for he had the courage to shoulder the blame for another man's crime." Oh, fellow citizens, I am weary of lies. They have poisoned every fibre of my being. You shall know everything. It was I who was guilty fifteen years ago.

MRS BERNICK (*quietly, emotionally*): Karsten!

MARTHA (*similarly*): Oh—Johan—!

MISS HESSEL: At last!

Dumb astonishment among the onlookers.

BERNICK: Yes, fellow citizens! I was the guilty one, and he was the one who fled. The false and evil rumours which were afterwards spread about him it is now too late to refute. But who am I to complain of this? Fifteen years ago I raised myself on these rumours. Whether they are now to bring me down is a question that each one of you must argue with his own conscience.

ROERLUND: What a thunderbolt! The town's foremost citizen! (*Softly, to* MRS BERNICK) Oh, Mrs Bernick, I feel most deeply sorry for you.

HILMAR: What an admission! Well, I must say—!

BERNICK: But you must not decide tonight. I beg each of you to return home to collect your thoughts and to look into your hearts. When you are calm again you will decide whether by speaking thus openly I have lost or won. Goodbye. I still have much to atone for; but that is between myself and my own conscience. Good night. Take away these trappings. This is not the time nor the place for them.

ROERLUND: I should think not indeed! (*Softly, to* MRS BERNICK) Run away! She was quite unworthy of me after all. (*Half-aloud to the Committee*) Well, gentlemen, after this I think we had better depart as quietly as we can.

HILMAR: How anyone is to wave the banner of ideals high after this I really—ugh!

The news meanwhile has been whispered from mouth to mouth.

The CROWD *drifts away.* RUMMEL, SANDSTAD *and* VIGELAND *also go, arguing in subdued but vehement tones.* HILMAR *wanders out right. Silence.*

BERNICK, MRS BERNICK, MARTHA, MISS HESSEL *and* KRAP *are left in the room.*

BERNICK: Betty, can you forgive me?

MRS BERNICK (*smiles*): Do you know, Karsten, this has been the happiest moment I have had for years?

BERNICK: What do you mean?

MRS BERNICK: For years now I have believed that you were once mine, but I had lost you. Now I know you were never mine; but I shall win you.

BERNICK (*throws his arms round her*): Oh, Betty, you have won me! Lona has taught me to understand for the first time what kind of woman you really are. But Olaf—Olaf!

MRS BERNICK: Yes, now you can see him. Mr Krap—

She talks quietly to KRAP *upstage. He goes out through the verandah door. During the following, all the transparencies, and the lights in the houses outside, are gradually extinguished.*

BERNICK (*quietly*): Thank you, Lona. You have saved what was best in me—and for me.

MISS HESSEL: What else do you think I wanted?

BERNICK: Yes—was it this you came back for—or was it something else? I don't understand you, Lona.

MISS HESSEL: Hm—

BERNICK: It wasn't hatred, then? And it wasn't revenge? Then why did you come back here?

MISS HESSEL: Old friendship doesn't rust, Karsten.

BERNICK: Lona!

MISS HESSEL: When Johan told me about that lie, I vowed to myself: "The hero of my youth shall stand free and true."

BERNICK: Lona, Lona! How little I have deserved this from you!

MISS HESSEL: Ah, Karsten! If we women demanded our deserts—!

BERNICK (*runs towards him*): Olaf!

OLAF: Father, I promise you I won't ever again—

BERNICK: Run away?

OLAF: Yes, yes, I promise, Father.

BERNICK: And I promise you, you shall never have cause to. From now on you shall be allowed to grow up, not as the heir to my life's work, but as one who has his own life's work awaiting him.

OLAF: And may I become anything I like?

BERNICK: Yes, you may.

OLAF: Thank you. Then I don't want to become a pillar of society.

BERNICK: Oh? Why not?

OLAF: I think it must be so dull.

BERNICK: You shall be yourself, Olaf. That is all that matters. As for you, Aune—

AUNE: I know, Mr Bernick. I'm dismissed.

BERNICK: We'll stay together, Aune. And please forgive me.

AUNE: What! But the ship didn't sail this evening—

BERNICK: She shall not sail tomorrow, either. I gave you too little time. The work must be attended to more thoroughly.

AUNE: It will, Mr Bernick. And with the new machines!

BERNICK: Good. But it must be done thoroughly and honestly. There is much in us which needs to be repaired thoroughly and honestly. Well, good night, Aune.

AUNE: Good night, Mr Bernick—and thank you. Thank you!

He goes out right.

MRS BERNICK: They have all gone now.

BERNICK: And we are alone. My name does not shine in letters of fire any longer. All the lights in the windows are out.

MISS HESSEL: Would you like them lit again?

BERNICK: Not for all the money in the world. Where have I been? You will be appalled when you know. I feel as though I had just returned to health and sanity after being poisoned.

But I feel it—I *can* become young and strong again. Oh, come closer, come closer around me! Come, Betty! Come, Olaf, my son! And you, Martha. Oh, Martha! It's as though I had never seen you all these years.

MISS HESSEL: I can well believe that. Your society is a society of bachelors. You don't notice the women.

BERNICK: True, true. And because of that—now I don't want any arguing, Lona—you must not leave Betty and me.

MRS BERNICK: No, Lona, you mustn't!

MISS HESSEL: How could I run away and abandon all you youngsters just when you're beginning to start a new life? Being a foster-mother is my job, isn't it? You and I, Martha—we two old maids—! What are you looking at?

MARTHA: How light the sky has grown! It's bright and calm over the sea. The *Palm Tree* has good luck in her sails.

MISS HESSEL: And good luck on board.

BERNICK: And we—we have a long, hard day ahead of us. I most of all. But let it come. Oh, gather close around me, you loyal and true women. That is something else I've learned in these past few days. It is you women who are the pillars of society.

MISS HESSEL: Then it's a poor wisdom you've learned, brother-in-law. (*Puts her hand firmly on his shoulder*) No, Karsten. The spirit of truth and the spirit of freedom—they are the pillars of society.

The Pillars of Society was the first play by Ibsen to be performed in England. In 1878, William Archer, then aged twenty-two, "dashed off a translation in less than a week," and contributed to the *Mirror of Literature* (2 March 1878) "a long and detailed analysis, with copious extracts."[1] Charles Archer, in his biography of his brother, has described how the play at last found its way on to the stage. "Having failed to find a publisher for his translation of *The Pillars of Society*, Archer had set himself, as the only way of bringing Ibsen to the front, to adapt the play for the English stage; for in those days it was unthinkable that a faithful translation, even of a French piece, much more of a play by an unknown Hyperborean dramatist, should ever make its way on to the London boards. By the end of 1878, an 'adaptation,' which might have been better described as an abridgement, had been accepted by Mr W. H. Vernon, who was much struck by the part of Consul Bernick. But Mr Vernon had no theatre at his disposal, and negotiations for a London production dragged on for nearly two years. At last, since no better might be, the piece was produced experimentally at a Gaiety matinée on 15 December 1880—and fell perfectly flat. The production, as a whole, was inevitably scrambling and ineffective. But the best setting and acting could not have made the play a success with the English critics and audiences of that day. Ibsen's time was not yet come."

This adaptation was entitled *Quicksands*.

[1] *William Archer*, by Charles Archer (London, 1931).

BERNICK	W. H. Vernon
SANSTED [*sic*]	Mr Vincent
ASTRUP [RUMMEL]	E. Girardot
NILSEN [VIGELAND]	Mr Freeman
JOHAN HESSEL [*sic*]	Arthur Dacre
HILMAR HESSEL [*sic*]	G. Canninge
DR BORCK [ROERLUND]	T. Balfour
KRUPP [KRAP]	G. Raiemond
HAUSEN [AUNE]	A. C. Hatton
OLAF	Master Arnold
MRS BERNICK	Miss M. A. Gifford
MARTHA	Fanny Addison
LONA HESSEL	Mrs Billington
DINA DORF	Cissy Grahame

Produced by W. H. Vernon

The performance was sympathetically noticed in *The Theatre*. After outlining the plot at length, the anonymous reviewer concluded: "Bernick's cold-blooded villainy appears somewhat inadequately punished. In this play, tentatively produced and fairly successful, Mr W. H. Vernon, Mrs Billington, Mr Arthur Dacre and Miss Cissey [*sic*] Grahame specially distinguished themselves."

Nine years later a revised version of the translation was presented, again for a single performance, as the main item[1] in a benefit matinée for Vera Beringer who, at the age of ten, appeared as the child Olaf. Despite the 1880 performance, the play was announced in the programme as being presented "for the first time in England." Elizabeth Robins made her first appearance in an Ibsen part, in the role of Martha. During the nine years since the Gaiety matinée, the only recorded performances of Ibsen in England had consisted of three productions of *A Doll's House : Breaking a Butterfly* (a

[1] "After the play, Mrs Kendal, for the only time this season, will recite *Ostler Joe*, and Mme Antoinette Sterling has kindly consented to sing *The Three Fishers*." (Note in the 1889 Opera Comique programme.)

free adaptation by Henry Arthur Jones and H. Herman) on 3 March 1884, two charity performances by "The Scribblers' Dramatic Society" (in aid of the Society for the Prevention of Cruelty to Children) in March 1885, and the important production of 7 June 1889 at the Novelty Theatre with Janet Achurch, Herbert Waring and Charles Charrington, described by Archer as "the first really effective performance of Ibsen in England."

Opera Comique, 17 *July* 1889

BERNICK	W. H. Vernon
MRS BERNICK	Mrs Davies
OLAF	Vera Beringer
MARTHA	Elizabeth Robins
JOHAN	J. G. Grahame
LONA HESSEL	Geneviève Ward
HILMAR	E. Hendrie
DR ROERLUND	John Beauchamp
RUMMEL	E. Smart
VIGELAND	E. Girardot
SANDSTAD	Mr Branscombe
DINA DORF	Annie Irish
KRAFT [KRAP]	G. Canninge
AUNE	A. Wood
MRS RUMMEL	Fanny Robertson
MRS HOLT	Miss St Ange
MRS LYNGE	Miss M. A. Giffard
MISS RUMMEL	May Beringer
MISS HOLT	Miss Braekstad

Produced by W. H. Vernon

"It is impossible in a short article to do justice to this remarkable play, in which Ibsen pours out his withering satire upon the lies and conventionalities of society. Not a line is inserted without a reason. All the characters are drawn with a master hand. Admirable as is the comedy vein of many of the scenes, the tragedy of others is no less admirable. Bernick's unconscious revelations of selfishness are marvellously true to nature, and Mr Vernon brought out the meaning of every syllable. . . . The half-chivalric, half-indifferent character of Johan Toennessen was excellently portrayed by Mr Grahame. . . . No one could have played Tona [*sic*] Hessel better than Miss Ward. We are accustomed to associate this admirable actress with parts of a cynical and hard nature, but in Tona Miss Ward had a tenderness, a lovingness and a womanliness which touched all hearts. . . . The minor parts were well filled."

R. K. Hervey in *The Theatre*

"The first and third acts certainly could bear much excision, but the second and fourth were received with acclamation, and the principals vociferously summoned. The piece, with its present cast, would in all probability succeed for a time in an evening bill, more particularly after the excitement and controversy the production of *A Doll's House* created."

Austin Brereton in *The Stage*

During 1890, the American actress Mrs Winslow gave solo readings of *The Pillars of Society* in various English cities. In 1901, the Stage Society revived the play for two matinées:

Strand Theatre, 12 May 1901[1]

BERNICK	Oscar Asche
MRS BERNICK	Annie Webster
OLAF	George Hersee
MARTHA	Mrs Charles Maltby
JOHAN	Albert Gran
TONA [*sic*] HESSEL	Constance Robertson
HILMAR	Bromley Davenport
DR ROERLUND	Charles Quartermaine

[1] The second matinee, to which the press were invited, was performed on the following afternoon, 13 May, at the Garrick Theatre.

RUMMEL	Dalziel Heron
VIGELAND	S. B. Brereton
SANDSTAD	A. H. Leveaux
DINA DORF	Dora Barton
KRAFT [KRAP]	D. J. Williams
AUNER [sic]	A. E. George
MRS RUMMEL	Lucy Franklein
MRS HOLT	Mabel Hardinge
MRS LYNGE	Sybil Ruskin
MISS RUMMEL	Helen Thurby
MISS HOLT	Ethel Marcus

Produced by Oscar Asche

"Ibsen, the author of *The Pillars of Society*, stands to Ibsen the creator of *Hedda Gabler* as Wagner of *Rienzi* faces Wagner of *Parsifal*. You know what the great master himself said to Professor Hagedorn, when the latter asked his opinion about *Rienzi*. 'Oh,' he said, 'that was written by the other Wagner'; and much the same applies to Ibsen. . . .

"*The Pillars of Society* was on the whole given with great credit to everybody concerned. My only objection to the performance was that more rehearsal would have been useful, and that in the cast a more careful observation of the ages of the various characters would have helped our imagination. . . . As we saw it before us, we could hardly believe it conceivable that Martha was young enough to be loved by Johan, whilst, on the other hand, suspicion arose that when Lona went to America with him, their relationship was not—well, brotherly. In plays of such magnitude as *The Pillars of Society* these apparent trifles grow to importance. . . . Mr Oscar Asche was not only the organizer of the performance, but also its life and soul in the personality of Consul Bernick. Mr Asche has done many good things, but none so ambitious, and none so successful, particularly in the first part. . . . It was a fine effort, worthy of a true artist."

J. T. Grein in the *Sunday Special*

"Ibsen here is, first and foremost, the rattling good playwright. Why this strong, ingenious, rattling good play of his has never been produced by a commercial manager is a mystery that I cannot fathom. . . . Superior persons may sneer at the play (especially its last act) as melodrama: but it is melodrama of the very best kind. It is a hustle of ingenious and exciting chances around strongly and truly delineated characters, and the comic relief (of which there is much) is real straightforward fun. The public would take to it like a duck to the water."

Max Beerbohm in the Saturday Review

Playhouse, Liverpool, 29 *January* 1913

BERNICK	Laurence Hanray
MRS BERNICK	Hazel Thompson
OLAF	Miss Trainer
MARTHA	Estelle Winwood
JOHAN	Grendon Bentley
LONA HESSEL	Aida Jenoure
HILMAR	Ernest Bodkin
DR ROERLUND	J. H. Roberts
RUMMEL	Oliver Johnston
VIGELAND	Dion Titheradge
SANDSTAD	John Garside
DINA DORF	Dorothy Day
KRAP	Miles Malleson
AUNE	Arthur Chesney
MRS RUMMEL	Louise Holbrooke
MRS HOLT	Dorothy Kingsley
MRS LYNGE	Marjorie Patterson
MISS RUMMEL	Jessie Neill
MISS HOLT	Miss Russel-Rogerson

Produced by Basil Dean

Repertory Theatre, Birmingham, 14 *September* 1918

BERNICK	Joseph A. Dodd
MRS BERNICK	Cathleen Orford

OLAF	Sidney Leon
MARTHA	Margaret Chatwin
JOHAN	H. Scott Sunderland
LONA HESSEL	Mary Raby
HILMAR	Arthur Claremont
DR ROERLUND	J. Adrian Byrne
RUMMEL	Reginald Gatty
VIGELAND	Arnold Ridley
SANDSTAD	Eric Ross
DINA DORF	Maud Gill
KRAP	Noel Shammon
AUNE	William J. Rea
MRS RUMMEL	Dorothy Massingham
MRS HOLT	Dorothy Taylor
MRS LYNGE	Alma Broadridge
MISS RUMMEL	Winifred Reader
MISS HOLT	Nancy Staples

Produced by John Drinkwater

Everyman Theatre, 13 *July* 1926

BERNICK	Charles Carson
MRS BERNICK	Barbara Everest
OLAF	Anne Bolt
MARTHA	Josephine Wilson
JOHAN	Michael Hogan
LONA HESSEL	Sybil Arundale
HILMAR	Brember Wills
DR ROERLUND	Milton Rosmer
RUMMEL	Charles Laughton
VIGELAND	J. Hubert Leslie
DINA DORF	Gwendolen Evans
KRAP	Gilbert Ritchie
AUNE	Orlando Barnett
MRS RUMMEL	Margaret Carter
MRS HOLT	Drusilla Wills
MRS LYNGE	Marie Wright

Produced by Milton Rosmer

"While the confession is still unmade, while the lie is still a lie, and a dozen others are suffering for it, how alive the struggle is, and how brilliant its climax! Mr Charles Carson makes of this climax, when the Consul confronts his townspeople and tells them the truth of himself, a deeply moving scene, and it is moving precisely in proportion to his earlier revelations of the man's character. But when it is done, when nothing remains but the quiet, concluding passages, ought not the emphasis to shift from him to the inconspicuous Martha? Miss Josephine Wilson plays this little part so well that it is a thousand pities that, through no fault of hers, Martha's final importance should be obscured. It is obscured partly because the stage is awkwardly grouped, partly because the noise of the others is allowed to tread down her quietness. There is, indeed, throughout the performance, a certain restless tendency to over-emphasize what needs only steadiness for its true effect. Miss Gwendolen Evans, Mr Orlando Barnett and Mr Michael Hogan are conspicuous exceptions, and there are several small sketches admirably done, but Miss Arundale leaps too quickly to extremes, Mr Brember Wills is a little lost in mannerism now and then, and even Mr Milton Rosmer is capable of lapses. But a good and stirring play it remains."

The Times

On 5 August 1926 the above production transferred to the Royalty Theatre. The cast was the same, with the following exceptions:

HILMAR	Charles Garry
DR ROERLUND	Felix Aylmer
RUMMEL	W. H. Dewhurst
VIGELAND	Hector Abbas
DINA DORF	Beatrix Thompson

BERNICK	John McCallum
MRS BERNICK	Margaret Vines
OLAF	Colin Gibson
MARTHA	Maureen Pryor
JOHAN	Michael Warre
LONA HESSEL	Valerie White
HILMAR	David Markham
DR ROERLUND	Charles Lloyd Pack
RUMMEL	Wensley Pithey
VIGELAND	John Dunbar
SANDSTAD	Jonathan Field
DINA DORF	Norah Gorsen
KRANT [KRAP]	Gerald Cross
AUNE	Beckett Bould
MRS RUMMEL	Nan Munro
MRS LYNGE	Ilona Ference

Produced by Stephen Harrison

NOTE ON THE TRANSLATION

The Pillars of Society is, like *A Doll's House* and *An Enemy of the People*, a fairly straightforward play to translate. The chief problems are Hilmar Toennessen and Lona Hessel. Hilmar talks in a fanciful manner, overloaded with adjectives and ridiculous flights of imagination, like Hjalmar Ekdal in *The Wild Duck*. Lona has a breezy, slangy way of speaking which contrasts markedly with the prim speech of the local stay-at-homes, and since she and Johan have spent the past fifteen years in America I have tried to make them talk like Americans.

The Norwegian word *samfund* can mean either society in general, or a specific community. Ibsen uses it in both senses, and I have translated it sometimes as society and sometimes as community, as the context demanded.

As a postscript one may remark that the chief characters in *The Pillars of Society* are a good deal younger than they are generally played. The "incident" with Dina's mother took place fifteen years ago. Johan was then nineteen, so he is now thirty-four. Bernick was then four years older than Johan, so he is thirty-eight. Martha is the same age as Johan. Mrs Bernick is older than her brother, so is presumably in her middle to late thirties; and Lona Hessel is older than Mrs Bernick and therefore presumably in her late thirties or early forties. She should not be more than a few years older than Bernick, if at all, since he nearly married her.

M.M.